RUSSIAN ENERGY POLITICS IN THE BALTICS, POLAND, AND UKRAINE

A NEW STEALTH IMPERIALISM?

Author
Keith C. Smith

December 2004

About CSIS

The Center for Strategic and International Studies (CSIS) is a nonprofit, bipartisan public policy organization established in 1962 to provide strategic insights and practical policy solutions to decisionmakers concerned with global security. Over the years, it has grown to be one of the largest organizations of its kind, with a staff of some 200 employees, including more than 120 analysts working to address the changing dynamics of international security across the globe.

CSIS is organized around three broad program areas, which together enable it to offer truly integrated insights and solutions to the challenges of global security. First, CSIS addresses the new drivers of global security, with programs on the international financial and economic system, foreign assistance, energy security, technology, biotechnology, demographic change, the HIV/AIDS pandemic, and governance. Second, CSIS also possesses one of America's most comprehensive programs on U.S. and international security, proposing reforms to U.S. defense organization, policy, force structure, and its industrial and technology base and offering solutions to the challenges of proliferation, transnational terrorism, homeland security, and post-conflict reconstruction. Third, CSIS is the only institution of its kind with resident experts on all the world's major populated geographic regions.

CSIS was founded four decades ago by David M. Abshire and Admiral Arleigh Burke. Former U.S. senator Sam Nunn became chairman of the CSIS Board of Trustees in 1999, and since April 2000, John J. Hamre has led CSIS as president and chief executive officer.

Headquartered in downtown Washington, D.C., CSIS is a private, tax-exempt, 501(c) 3 institution. CSIS does not take specific policy positions; accordingly, all views expressed herein should be understood to be solely those of the author(s).

Library of Congress Cataloging-in-Publication Data
CIP information available on request.
ISBN 0-89206-456-0

The CSIS Press
Center for Strategic and International Studies
1800 K Street, N.W., Washington, D.C. 20006
Tel: (202) 887-0200
Fax: (202) 775-3199
E-mail: books@csis.org
Web: http://www.csis.org/

Contents

Preface

Imperialism. Colonialism. Dominion. These terms are often used to describe the past century of Moscow's foreign policy, whether Czarist, Soviet, or post Soviet. Those who have lived in Russia's shadow since 1991 have had to grapple with these emotionally charged terms when they attempt to describe the motivations of the power elites in Moscow and their ideas concerning Russia's relationships with its neighbors who were so recently under the Kremlin's control. Finding the appropriate word is equally challenging today when one attempts to describe Russia's projection of its energy power in the five countries—Estonia, Latvia, Lithuania, Poland, and Ukraine—that are the subjects of this study.

Whether for reasons of national security or national insecurity, many of Russia's elites have viewed their country's size and wealth of natural resources as an instrument with which to exert or reexert control over those countries that were formally or informally part of the Soviet empire. The end of the Cold War did not erase from the minds of many Russian policymakers the historical desire to project power for its own sake and create a Russia that is strong internally and respected internationally.

This attitude persists among Russian elites; and since Vladimir Putin replaced Boris Yeltsin, a national security policy emphasizing greater power projection has been systematically and skillfully implemented in the entire post-Soviet region, with greatest success in Ukraine. Putin made restoring Russian power and influence a personal priority—not a surprising preference because strength and respect are contained in the national security policy papers of all major countries. A disturbing trend over the past two years, with serious implications for the neighborhood, however, has been Putin's successful move to consolidate state control over the Russian energy sector and eliminate any competing source of influence that might come from privatized energy firms. This policy is strikingly similar to the success Putin has experienced in curbing opposition within the media, political parties, and non-governmental organizations. He has also reversed some of the earlier progress made in the democratization of Russia. Putin's reassertion of control over the energy industry has made it easier for him to use energy as an instrument by which to project state influence and control over the countries of East Central Europe.

Putin's policies only confirm that developing a "normal" relationship with Moscow will at best be a long and difficult process for countries tied to Russia for the past half century. Russia's historic intellectual and institutional separation from the Westernized international security community has produced a national ethos unlikely to entrust national security to multilateral or regional organizations. Foreign policy, like domestic policy, is too often viewed in zero-sum terms by Russia's elites.

For understandable reasons, East Central Europeans have reason to fear Russia because of its unique geographical position, its well-established willingness to use military power against its neighbors, and the world's increasing dependence on Russia's natural resources. Although the enlargement of the North Atlantic Treaty Organization (NATO) and the European Union (EU) have altered the traditional power advantage of Russia, all of Russia's Western neighbors continue to live in the shadow of the world's second-best-armed nuclear state—one that has been moving back toward authoritarianism.

Some will argue that Russian economic behavior in the Near Abroad is not a serious threat to the sovereignty of Russia's smaller neighbors. This monograph attempts to persuade readers that the risks are larger than generally recognized and the issue demands greater attention from the United States and Western Europe.

This project developed as a result of earlier studies of Russian-Baltic relations and, particularly, the actions of Russian companies in the Baltics from 1992 to 2000. Information developed regarding the special relationship between Russian energy companies and influential business leaders in Central Europe as well as from a recognition that many of the difficulties faced by the new democracies in the Baltic states, Poland, and Ukraine stem from their dependence on Russian energy sources.

The winter of 1992–1993 was particularly cold in Estonia, Latvia, and Lithuania. At that time, the Yeltsin government was using an energy cutoff in an attempt to effect policy change in the three countries. Moscow publicly justified the disruption as necessary owing to the alleged unwillingness of these three countries to pay for oil in hard currency and at world market prices—an effective fourfold increase in energy costs. It is no coincidence that the oil cutoff immediately followed demands by the Baltic states that Moscow remove all Russian troops from their countries. Many Latvians and Estonians were forced, because of Russia's energy embargo, to endure cold nights in unheated apartments and homes. Moscow also intended the cutoff as a warning to non-Baltic former republics of the USSR to think hard before defying Russia on economic or security policy.

During 1998–1999, U.S. officials in Lithuania watched with dismay as Transneft, Russia's state oil transport company, cut off oil shipments to Lithuania on nine separate occasions. Each interruption was an attempt to force Lithuania to cede control of its oil pipelines, refinery, and port terminal to LUKOIL, ostensibly a private firm but one that was and still remains an instrument of Kremlin policy. On each occasion, Transneft and LUKOIL justified the cut, citing technical or supply problems. Although the disruptions lasted from one day to several weeks, each disruption signaled the Russian government's willingness to strong-arm its neighbors almost a decade after the breakup of the Soviet Union and the diplomatic recognition by the Kremlin in August 1991 of the independent Baltic states.

During an extremely tense period of negotiations between LUKOIL and the U.S. energy company, Williams Companies, Inc., in October 1999, Russia's Ministry of Foreign Affairs suddenly replaced its ambassador to Lithuania with a 25-year veteran of the KGB, in order to assist LUKOIL in behind-the-scenes efforts to influence Lithuania's government and the public. This was the first time in post–Cold War Central Europe that any government had assigned a high-level intelligence officer as an ambassador in order to support a commercial negotiation.

It has become increasingly apparent that the most prosperous individuals in many of the former Communist countries were those with direct or indirect ties to Russia's energy industry. Most Western observers are familiar with the acquisition of much of Russia's energy assets by a few private individuals, during what has been referred to as "the sale of the century." Fewer, however, are aware of the enormous financial advantages that many Central Europeans acquired through informal relationships with Russia's current and former intelligence apparatus and with Russian industrial leaders. These ties allowed such non-Russians to become intermediaries for Russian energy companies and to share massive quick profits that came from exploiting energy price differentials between Russia and the rest of Europe.

This monograph attempts to create as accurate a picture as possible of Russia's use of its energy power and the political and security risks that this substantial power, if unchecked, poses for the creation of a Europe whole and free. Separate studies within CSIS cover Russia's energy relationship with the countries of the Caucasus and Central Asia. Although the new "great game," which involves competition between Russia and the West in those two regions, directly influences the economic prospects of the countries of East Central Europe, events in the Caucasus and Central Asia will be mentioned in this study only as they deal directly with Russia's energy influence over political and security developments in Estonia, Latvia, Lithuania, Poland, and Ukraine.

Most of the current literature on the breakup of the USSR in August 1991 focuses on the difficult transformation of Russia and of the many countries and nationalities previously held in the grip of the Kremlin. It is understandable that much of the Western press has swung, at times quickly, between optimism and pessimism in its coverage of political trends in Moscow. The same swings exist in respect to prospects for the establishment of democracy and market economies in East Central Europe. The enrichment of a few oligarchs in Russia, the chaos of post-Soviet societies, and the tensions with the West are still analyzed at length. Not enough attention, however, has been devoted to the unique set of opportunities that the breakup of the Soviet Union has given to former Communist leaders outside Russia, in both the former Soviet Union and Warsaw Pact countries.

The intent of this paper is not to condemn the Russian government for supporting the foreign commercial interests of its energy companies. All countries strive to extend their own influence and that of their companies in other parts of the world. The United States and the countries of Western Europe have historically acted in an imperialistic fashion in the Middle East to promote their energy interests, and Western energy companies still occasionally engage in activities in West Africa that should not be tolerated by the international community. Russian control of the energy infrastructure in neighboring states and Moscow's attempt to maintain monopoly control of pipelines that bring oil and gas from the Caspian region to Western markets are understandable in a region where win-lose (not win-win) is a deeply rooted business principle.

Nonetheless, Western leaders no longer systematically use their companies to influence or undermine democratically elected governments. Western firms are also required to open their books to international scrutiny. Most Russian energy companies avoid adopting current international business standards that would require them to engage in greater transparency, domestically and overseas. Russia imposes no penalties on companies that interfere in foreign elections and corrupt foreign officials. Russia does not have a U.S.-style foreign corrupt practices act. Nor does Moscow yet accept that it should develop a more level playing field for both domestic and foreign firms in order to attract greater foreign investment and promote an open society. Not enough Russians understand that, to be viewed internationally as a normal society, their neighbors must feel more confidence in dealing with the Kremlin's leadership and with foreign branches of Russian enterprises.

There is some irony in that Russian leaders have learned well some of the lessons of capitalism. When foreign laws do not curb monopoly or oligopoly power, Russian business leaders will often gain substantial control of the market and develop influence over local politics. Transparency in government and respect for property rights remain weak in East Cental Europe. These factors, combined with the strains and opportunities of nation building, create opportunities for rapacious capitalism and neocolonialism on the part of Russia's leadership.

Therefore, the United States and the EU should vigorously hold the Russian government and its national companies accountable when they endanger the development of democracy and open markets in those neighboring states where they are doing business. The international community should support efforts by the importing countries to resist the actions of Russian firms that promote corrupt international business practices. The West should more actively counter moves by Russian monopolies to deny markets and investment opportunities to those firms not playing by international standards. And, most important, the West has an obligation to become involved when the Russian government uses its companies to advance Russian national security policies that threaten the security interests of its weaker neighbors and the international community at large.

In preparation for this study, the author conducted more than 100 interviews with energy and political specialists in Russia, Poland, Ukraine, Estonia, Latvia, Lithuania, Scandinavia, and the United States. Because of the sensitivity of the subject matter, interviewees' names have been omitted. Most individuals were understandably reluctant to talk freely if cited by name. Therefore, information regarding the identities of those interviewed has been given only to the sponsors of the project, including the Center for Strategic and International Studies.

To CSIS and the foundations that have supported this project, this author owes an enormous debt for their faith in my ability to pull together this sensitive but complex subject. The project would not have proceeded without financial support from the Smith Richardson Foundation and the Stuart Family Foundation. For their help on research subjects, thanks are extended to Elisabeth Zentos, Anastasia Handy, Nathan Puffer, Tiffany Casey, Kristin Padgett, and Anna Kolesnichenko. Of course, the support of Celeste Wallander, director of the CSIS Russia and Eurasia Program, was instrumental in my taking on this project in the first place.

The above individuals should not be held responsible for either the very subjective analysis contained in this paper or the recommendations submitted to policymakers. The analysis and conclusions reflect only the author's opinions and prejudices.

Executive Summary

The policies of the Putin government pose a significant challenge to the development of transparent democratic governments and free markets in those countries that are dependent on Russia for their energy resources. Ever since the collapse of the Soviet Union, the Kremlin has used its energy monopoly to influence non-economic policies in the neighboring countries of Estonia, Latvia, Lithuania, Poland, and Ukraine.

The five countries along Russia's western borders are tied to Russia by Soviet and post-Soviet-era pipelines, rail lines and refineries. Because Russia enjoys a near monopoly of energy supplies to East Central Europe, the Kremlin possesses powerful leverage with which to regain control of the existing infrastructure in the neighboring democratic states. Even absent neighboring countries' long, historic dependence on Russian technology and infrastructure, geography alone dictates that Russia will likely remain the nearest and least costly supplier of oil and gas to East Central Europe. In addition, the West's growing dependence on imported energy resources only exacerbates the difficulties confronting the quest by the five countries for alternative supplies.

Russia's national security interest, as defined by Putin and a large part of the power structure, is to reestablish Moscow's control over strategic infrastructure in neighboring states. This control is to be used to ensure that friendly governments are in place to support Russian security and economic interests. It would be an exaggeration to call Russian economic power projection by itself imperialism, but the neocolonial characteristics of Russia's foreign energy policy are readily apparent to those living in the immediate neighborhood.

The energy industry is crucial to Russia's ability to create wealth and to close the gap with the West, which gives those who own or control resource assets enormous advantages in the struggle for power inside of Russia. This struggle is complicated by the lack of clear and enforceable commercial law, a corrupt bureaucracy, and a lack of transparency in the political-industrial complex. Although the problem of corruption in the five countries would exist independent of Russia, the problem is exacerbated by the policies of the Kremlin and its most powerful ministries, including the intelligence services. Moscow uses its intelligence assets and its ties with wealthy members of the economic elite (and former leaders of the Soviet-era *nomenklatura*) in East Central Europe to supplement the monopoly power of its energy supply relationship.

Russia's attempts to strong-arm its neighbors by cutting off energy supplies started as early as its attempt in 1990 to crush the independence movement in the Baltic states, and they have continued to the present time. The latest cutoff of energy supplies—in May 2004—was directed against Belarus, but it also affected Poland and Lithuania.

The larger political issues surrounding the Kremlin's destruction of YUKOS, its most innovative and transparent energy company, should give pause to those in the West who have looked at YUKOS as a unique case in which the Russian state is merely confiscating the illegally secured assets of one of its best-known oligarchs. The whole affair is a timely demonstration of President Putin's view that Russia's natural resources must be used as much to advance narrowly defined national security interests as to improve the general standard of living.

The United States has not had a well-formulated policy focused on countering the dubious business practices of Russia's energy companies. Nor has much attention been paid to the growing potential for these firms and the Kremlin to undermine the new political and economic systems that emerged from the collapse of Communism in East Central Europe. U.S. policymakers have vigorously supported the efforts of U.S. companies to enter the markets as competitors or partners to Russian companies, but the U.S. government has failed to develop policies that would help its Central European allies minimize the economic and security risks of Russian energy domination.

EU enlargement and the debate surrounding a new EU constitution have diverted the European Commission's attention from some of the critical issues still confronting the new democratic states to the east. Individual European governments also still prefer to deal with Russia in a bilateral, rather than multilateral, context; and interest in East Central Europe by some Western governments has actually declined recently.

If Russia were clearly on its way toward an open, transparent, and modern democratic state, with ethical corporate behavior enforced by an honest judiciary, the problems outlined in this paper would quickly fade. A more democratic Russia would more likely respect the sovereignty and aspirations of it neighbors.

Nevertheless, an early transformation is not in the cards. The three Baltic states, Poland, and Ukraine will have to adopt new domestic policies and invest considerable resources of their own in order to ensure a greater degree of energy independence. Countries such as Ukraine and Lithuania must decide on the degree of ownership control they will cede to Russian oil and gas interests. A greater degree of political and financial transparency in all five countries might also prevent Russian energy companies from influencing decisions on privatization or the sale of energy facilities through the use of campaign contributions and under-the-table payments to local political leaders. The United States should take the lead in working with the EU and the Central Europeans to better understand the political and security risks that stem from Russia's use of its energy companies as instruments of foreign policy. The consolidation of transparent democracy and open markets in East Central Europe would have a significantly positive impact on the course of reform in Russia, Belarus, and Ukraine. Therefore, it is in the long-term security interests of the United States and its allies to break the cycle of corruption and political influence that underlie Russia's foreign energy policy in Estonia, Latvia, Lithuania, Poland, and Ukraine.

Map of Russian Oil and Gas Pipeline Complex

Source: U.S. Government.

CHAPTER 1

The Setting

Russian–Eastern European Relations after the Breakup of the USSR

The Russia of 2004 is in many ways a vastly different country from the Soviet Union of 1990. The Communist Party of the Russian Federation is but a pale reflection of the monolithic machine that ruled not only the largest country in the world but also an incredibly diverse empire embracing Eurasia and almost all of Central Europe. Today, however, the West often fears the political and security consequences of Russia's economic and military weakness as much as it fears Russia's potential strength. Although Russia's current gross domestic product (GDP) equals only that of Belgium or of Los Angeles County, California, Russia's GDP is growing at over 7 percent annually; unfortunately, however, the development of its economy is not leading to greater democracy or a weakening of imperial or colonial impulses.

Russian pressure has not been uniformly successful. It is worth noting that Poland, as the largest and most important Western part of the former Soviet empire, was not deterred by Russian opposition to its integration into European and transatlantic institutions. To the relief of many in Brussels, once Poland joined the North Atlantic Treaty Organization (NATO) in 1999, Poland's relations with Moscow markedly improved. The Kremlin belatedly recognized that it was shortsighted to continue its opposition to Poland's inclusion into Western institutions. Poland's size and geographical position were just too important to Russia's economic relations with the rest of Europe for Russia to antagonize a generation of Poles.

Poles, unlike many Ukrainians, had at no time during the past century resigned themselves to being a part of Russia or the Soviet empire. Indeed, Polish history is replete with details of suffering at the hands of czarist Russia and then Communist Russia. By the early 1990s, Poland was too big, too stubborn, and already too integrated into the West for Russian intimidation to have much effect. Polish policy toward Russia during the 1990s was a mixture of firm adherence to a policy of integration into European and transatlantic institutions. At the same time, Poles sought to reassure Moscow that Poland understood Russia's need for international respect and for closer economic relations with the West.

The Baltic states, on the other hand, felt more threatened by Moscow than did Poland or Ukraine. From 1994 to 2001, Moscow repeatedly warned NATO not to enlarge to include those countries behind a hypothetical "red line" that included any territory once part of the Soviet Union. Russia's foreign and defense ministries appeared to believe that this bluster would keep the Baltic states out of the North Atlantic alliance. Moscow hoped that its refusal to sign border agreements with the

Baltic states and its railing against alleged human rights violations against ethnic Russians by Latvians and Estonians would prevent a majority of NATO members from supporting Baltic membership in NATO. The Balts' determination to join the alliance only intensified following repeated claims by Moscow that the Baltic states voluntarily joined the Soviet Union in 1940. As late as June 2000, the Russian Ministry of Foreign Affairs stated that "the USSR sent its troops into the Baltic region [in 1940] only after the leaders there requested it," and Deputy Foreign Minister Ivan Sergeyev restated this position in March 2001.[1]

Moscow's actions could not have been better designed to push the West and the Baltic states together. Russian pressure only spurred on the Baltic states and their supporters, such as the United States, Poland, Norway, and Denmark, to bring these countries under NATO's security umbrella. In the end, the Kremlin's repeated threats of unspecified retaliation if NATO crossed over the red line proved to be hollow, and the successful second round of enlargement only embarrassed the Kremlin and added to Russian humiliation.

NATO no longer considers Russia to be a military threat to Europe. When the Baltic states and five other countries joined NATO in April 2004, only four F-16s from alliance members symbolically patrolled the skies over Estonia, Latvia, and Lithuania. Even as the alliance is enlarging, it dedicates more time than ever trying to enlist Russian support for NATO's security agenda. Indeed, many in the West believe that it is Russia's feeling of weakness that hinders greater NATO-Russia cooperation. This is a flawed thesis, however, because Russian elites are inclined to believe in the exceptionalism of their country's values, a belief that prevents Russia from submitting its policies to the scrutiny of international institutions.

Ukraine, on the other hand, is considered by Russians, and some in Ukraine as well, to be an accident of history. If Nikita Khrushchev had not been from the Ukraine region, if he had not ceded territory from the Russian Republic to the Ukrainian Republic, or if Stalin had not insisted that Ukraine be considered an independent country in terms of membership in the United Nations (UN), there might never have been an independent Ukraine. Most Russians consider Ukraine to be the heart of Slavic Russia and cannot seem to absorb the fact that so many people living within Ukraine's borders should favor independent relations with the West, let alone claim the right to reject Moscow's leadership on European security issues.

All five countries covered by this study differ quite fundamentally from each other, and each pursues its own unique relationship with Russia.

- Estonia, the smallest of the five, has been the most aggressive in telling Moscow to stay out of its affairs.

- Latvia, experiencing continued Russian hostility over its alleged poor handling of its large ethnic Russian population, has suffered a unique set of problems at Russian hands.

- Lithuania, with its relatively small ethnic Russian population, has dealt with Moscow most confidently of the three Baltic states.

---

1. Mark Kramer, "Why Is Russia Still Peddling This Old Soviet Lie?" *Washington Post*, June 10, 2001, p. B2.

- Poland, except in the area of energy policy, feels relatively confident in its own dealings with Russia, but it worries that its security could be compromised if Ukraine and Belarus become increasingly dependent on Moscow or if Poland's eastern border becomes the line dividing "two Europes."

- Ukraine, the largest of the five countries with 50 million people, is the least likely to challenge Moscow. A constant debate goes on regarding relations with the West, but the Ukrainian leadership under Leonid Kuchma conspired with Russian interests to divide up much of the country's economic infrastructure. In consequence, Kyiv is the capital where Russian representatives exercise the greatest influence. Hosting a former Russian prime minister and energy czar as ambassador is both a source of pride and concern for Ukrainians.

Russia's Continued Quest for Empire

The formal breakup of the Soviet Union in August 1991 brought relief in the West and joy to those who had for so long been forced to submit to the Kremlin's control. In Russia, however, it created a deep sense of national humiliation within the Russian populace and sincere apprehension about the future. The psychological trauma of losing an empire, particularly in a country so recently feared by much of the world, should not be discounted. The Russian intelligentsia had known since at least the 1960s that they were significantly poorer than those living to the west of them, including those residing in the satellite states of the Warsaw Pact. The intelligentsia understood early on that Russia was respected more for its vast military force and nuclear arsenal than for its living standards, its culture, or its political system. Yet Russians could always console themselves with the thought that they lived in a country that spanned 11 time zones and controlled countries as important as the German Democratic Republic, Poland, and Hungary and regions as rich as Ukraine and Kazakhstan.

Even as late as 1990, however, few Russians could imagine that large parts of the Soviet Union such as Kazakhstan and Turkmenistan, let alone Ukraine, would demand independence. For most Russians, therefore, the breakup of the Soviet Union does not qualify as a simple divorce but instead goes right to the heart of their national self-esteem. It is understandable in this light why Mikhail Gorbachev is respected by only a small minority of Russians and why President Vladimir Putin gains support by using the symbols of the Soviet Union as he visibly restores Russian influence in the former republics. As late as 2000, polls showed that a majority of Moscow's high school students would like to see the return of the Soviet Union or at least something approximating the empire of the czars.[2] In February 2004, President Putin stated that the collapse of the Soviet Union "is a national tragedy of an enormous scale."[3] His statement reflects the majority view in Russia.

---

2. Dmitri Trenin, *The End of Eurasia: Russia on the Border between Geopolitics and Globalization* (Washington, D.C.: Carnegie Endowment for International Peace, 2002), 37.

3. "Putin Says Collapse of USSR National Tragedy," Interfax, February 12, 2004.

Perhaps the fact that a majority of Russians still have a positive view of Joseph Stalin is, in part, a result of Stalin's success at extending Moscow's control beyond that of the czars. Power over others may seem like a poor substitute for democracy and a higher standard of living, but Russians have never had the advantage of being able to choose one over the other.

Russian history is replete with foreign invasions from the east, west, and south, and the country's political leaders have always exploited the fear of invasion from abroad to strengthen central authority and to cow Russians into submission. A unique brand of national paranoia has been nurtured through constant warnings about foreign invaders and exacerbated by nearly 70 years of isolation from the outside world. Even the horrific suffering of the Russian people in World War II was ascribed to the alleged connivance of Western governments with Hitler's Germany. The killing of so much of Russia's officer class by Stalin as well as Stalin's refusal to accept intelligence reports of an impending German invasion are today still absent from many Russian textbooks. Unlike Germany, which was occupied by the Allies after World War II and thereby forced to reexamine its history, Russia has not yet had to conduct a national reassessment of its imperial past.

The Russian Orthodox Church has traditionally played a strong role in reinforcing autocracy, if not totalitarianism. The Reformation that played a decisive part in weakening the political power of state-connected religions in the West never reached Russia. Today, the leadership of the Orthodox Church is again becoming a willing instrument of state policy and has intervened several times in support of President Putin's reelection and his domestic and foreign policies.

The patriarch is in the process of returning the church to its traditional role of promoting order and control in preference to democracy and Western values. The church sees competing religions, particularly the Roman Catholic Church, and vigorous democracy as serious threats to order and stability in Russia. It would be a mistake to underestimate the role of the Russian Orthodox Church in promoting the view that Moscow has a clear interest in dominating as much territory and as many people as possible.

Of course, Russians have as much right as any people to enhance national security and promote their culture, religion, and views on economic and political structures. Throughout the distinctive history of Russia, however, Russian national security has typically been at the expense of someone else's freedom. While today's Russia is regarded as more democratic than authoritarian by many observers in the West, it is viewed with utmost suspicion by those living in its neighborhood. Unless or until Russia develops more political and economic transparency and a culture of tolerance, it poses a potential threat to those living in its shadow, especially the five countries of this study.

CHAPTER 2

Energy Dependence and Political Independence

Pipelines Replace Red Lines

It is the thesis of this paper that current Russian policies pose a threat to the development of transparent democratic governments and free-market policies in those countries that depend on Russia for their energy resources. In today's modern industrial societies, energy resources are seen increasingly as a source of political and economic power. Furthermore, in this post–Cold War period, energy is more easily deployable for power projection than are nuclear weapons.

The countries currently most dependent on Russia for energy were part of the Soviet Union and the Warsaw Pact. For at least 50 years, all decisions regarding the pattern of industrialization and the intensity of energy use in the Soviet republics and in Warsaw Pact countries were made in Moscow. The Soviet Union pursued autarkic economic policies, although during the 1980s it developed a greater appetite for hard-currency exports. The economics of energy use were less important in the Communist system than were production volumes and the weaving together of all the affected countries into a unified economic system.

Ukraine, Estonia, Latvia, and Lithuania are, in varying degrees, especially tied to Russia by Soviet-era pipelines, rail lines, and refineries. Because Russia enjoys a near monopoly of energy supplies to East Central Europe (here defined as those countries east of the German, Austrian, and Italian borders), the Kremlin possesses powerful leverage with which to regain control of the existing infrastructure in neighboring democratic states. Refineries in these countries were designed to process heavy Russian crude oil and power plants to use gas from Russian fields. Even if the long, historic dependence of these areas on Russian technology and infrastructure is discounted, geography alone dictates that Russia will likely remain the nearest and cheapest supplier of oil and gas to East Central Europe. In some respects, Western Europe's growing dependence on imported energy resources only exacerbates the difficulties confronting the five countries' quest for alternative supplies.

Until recently, some benefits accrued to Estonia, Latvia, Lithuania, Poland, and Ukraine by reason of their proximity to Russia. For the most part, these countries could buy their natural gas or crude oil at prices well below world market levels. The Baltic states, for example, until recently paid about $80 for 1,000 cubic meters of gas and Poland paid about $108; some countries in Western Europe pay up to $120–$130. The price advantages for the Baltic states will likely end in 2005. In June

2004, sources in Russia's monopoly gas company, Gazprom,[4] announced that the Baltic states would also have to pay the same $120 that Germany pays. Now that Gazprom effectively controls the gas distribution systems in the three countries, it is easier to make price increases stick. Gazprom can also now prevent potential competitors from supplying gas to the neighborhood. Ukraine will likely continue to be treated by Moscow as a special case, and Moscow will continue to supply Ukraine with gas priced at $80 for 1,000 cubic meters. This could change if a future government in Kyiv more actively pursues NATO membership or supports pipeline routes that bypass Russia.

Nevertheless, the ready access to Russian oil and gas can be an advantage to the Baltic states and Poland, but only if Russian companies—now acting as instruments of Russian state policy—desist in the future from working to limit the sovereignty of the commercial partner. However, this would require the Russian government and Russian energy companies such as Transneft, LUKOIL, TNK, YUKOS, and Gazprom to free the Baltic states and Poland from a culture in which international business and politics is viewed in zero-sum terms. Present trends in Russian energy policy, however, do not lead to optimism regarding the Kremlin's behavior in the Central European countries.

Under present conditions, both Lithuania and Ukraine depend on Russia for almost 100 percent of their oil supply as well as for the majority of their natural gas imports. With this degree of dependence on Russian imports, it is no surprise that Russian companies are able to play such a decisive role in the two countries' economies. In the past Lithuania and Ukraine paid oil and gas prices lower than countries to their west paid, in part because Russia did not have alternative export routes to West European markets readily available. With the opening of additional export routes and markets, these advantages are not as great as they were a few years ago. In addition, as Gazprom buys into Baltic gas distribution systems, it is able to control availability as well as price.

Political Implications

The crucial issue is the impact this Russian dominance has or will have on the political and economic fabric of the five countries. Will Russian dominance reinforce or undermine the development of democratic governance? Will the less-transparent business practices and political clout of Russian companies significantly offset the more open, market-oriented societies promoted by the European Union (EU) and the United States? Will Russia be successful in using its energy leverage to undermine the security commitment of Poland and the Baltic states to the West? Is Ukraine capable of developing an open, transparent, Western-oriented society as long as Russian energy companies finance the political fortunes of the country's most corrupt business clans?

---

4. In 1989, Gazprom (Gazovaya Promyshlenost´, or Gas Industry) was founded through the of Gas Industry. A 1992 presidential decree and a 1993 resolution by the Council of Ministers of the Russian Federation transformed Gazprom into a joint stock company, after which the state continued to be the major shareholder.

The massive power of the Russian energy industry is evidenced by its ability to acquire ownership or control of pipelines, refineries, oil ports, distribution companies, retail gas stations, and power stations in most of the countries of East Central Europe in the space of seven or eight years, at a pace that has increased significantly since the election of Vladimir Putin to the presidency. Ownership usually has been accomplished by outright purchase or by a joint venture with local and international partners. The Russian energy company usually initiates this process by buying a blocking minority in the local company.

A good example of this is Gazprom's minority stake in the natural gas companies of Estonia, Latvia, and Lithuania. If it follows its usual pattern, Gazprom will later buy out other investors and thereby end up with majority control over the company's board of directors. Gazprom (or LUKOIL or TNK) gains effective control of a company by having a majority (or blocking minority) financial stake and by being the sole supplier of the raw material. When this combination is in place, the importing company has considerable room to raise prices and to keep any potential business rival out of the market. In some cases, to gain minority ownership the Russian company may need a Western business partner. Gazprom has effectively used partnership deals with Germany's Ruhrgas to gain equity footholds in the Baltic states and Poland.

In Lithuania, which is less energy independent than the other Baltic states even though it is now a member of the EU and has signed the EU's Energy Charter, YUKOS holds a majority stake in the oil pipeline from the Belarus border to the Baltic Sea. YUKOS also has majority control over the oil port of Butinge, as well as over the refinery at Mazeikiai, the largest facility in the Baltics.[5] LUKOIL owns the most extensive network of service stations. Gazprom has effective control of the country's monopoly natural gas company and also owns the Kaunas power plant that supplies energy to the country's second-largest city. Gazprom is also negotiating to purchase the country's Kronas hydroelectric plant, and it is

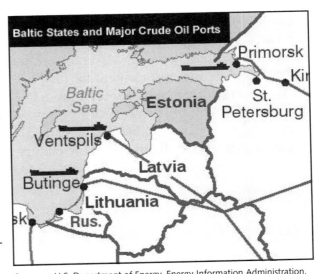

Source: U.S. Department of Energy, Energy Information Administration.

angling to acquire the country's largest electrical power generation unit at Elektrinai, near Vilnius. The Russian nuclear industry is the monopoly supplier of fuel

---

5. YUKOS was formed in 1993 by Russian government decree combining the oil producer Yuganskneftegas, the refining concern KuibyshevnefteOrgSintez, and several other distribution elements. YUKOS remained state owned until the troubled enterprise was privatized in 1996 in a series of tenders and auctions, making it Russia's first fully privatized oil company. As of late 2004, it appeared that YUKOS-Lithuania would end up in the hands of the newly merged Gazprom-Rosneft company or of LUKOIL.

rods to the two nuclear power reactors at Ignalina in northeast Lithuania. These nuclear plants supply 80 percent of Lithuania's electricity.

In Ukraine, four of the country's six oil refineries are majority owned by Russian companies. These four refineries are by the far the largest and most important in the country, accounting for up to 80 percent of Ukraine's refining capacity. Russian firms control companies that export almost 100 percent of Ukraine-produced oil products. These refined products go to nearby markets of Romania, Hungary, Bulgaria, and Slovakia. LUKOIL owns the oil port facilities as well as the refinery at Odessa, giving that company a key industrial complex with access to the Black Sea. The Odessa complex may someday also be a major pipeline link with Western and Central Europe, thereby giving a Russian state company control over that route as well.

A Ukrainian economist and adviser to the government stated in private that "no Ukrainian can give a flat refusal to LUKOIL, Gazprom or Transneft or to anyone with a close personal relationship to Putin." He claimed that at present Chubais and his Unified Energy System of Russia (UES)[6] are not close to Putin and can still be held by Ukraine at arm's length. Nevertheless, very few Ukrainian officials would support an energy policy that is seen as anti-Russian because Ukraine's business elite benefits economically from the close relationship with Russia. One Ukrainian consultant in the field of power and energy stated, "Our relationship is mutually beneficial. Russia gives Ukraine an advantageous price on gas, and Ukraine charges Russia relatively low transit fees." He added that it was "safer" not to comment on the political implications of this symbiotic relationship.

The Ukrainian presidential election in late 2004 gave Putin and Russia's energy companies additional political leverage because the ruling party in Ukraine desperately wanted Putin's endorsement for their preferred candidate.[7] The August 2004, 15-year energy agreement between President Leonid D. Kuchma of Ukraine and President Putin bound Ukraine's economy ever closer to Russia. In sum, Ukraine's energy industry, like its military-industrial complex, is increasingly becoming an appendage of Russian firms and the Kremlin's industrial and security policies.[8]

---

6. UES was founded by a resolution of the Russian Federation State Committee for Government Property Management in 1992, combining the largest subdivisions of electrical energy production and gaining 49 percent of shares in the few remaining regional utilities. A federal wholesale energy market was created and interregional energy unification continues. The effective electrical monopoly continues to be state run, with the government of the Russian Federation maintaining a 52 percent stake.

7. NTV Moscow, BBC Monitoring Service, August 18, 2004.

8. Robert Legvold and Celeste Wallander, eds., *Swords and Sustenance: The Economics of Security in Belarus and Ukraine* (Cambridge: MIT Press, 2003), 152–153.

CHAPTER 3

Power and the Energy Colossus

The Energy Sector in Russia's Economy

Twenty years ago, only a few foreigners specializing in Russia focused on the enormous energy export potential of the Soviet Union. Reliable information was hard to come by. Until the Arab oil embargo of 1973, few were interested in the possibility of Soviet oil replacing Middle East oil in European or U.S. markets. By the mid-1980s, however, the USSR had become the largest oil producer in the world, with peak production at 12.5 million barrels per day in 1988[9] and exports of more than 4.09 million barrels per day.[10] The outside world recognizes that Russia is a serious competitor to Saudi Arabia and the other Persian Gulf states. Russia's current proven oil reserves are estimated to be a substantial percentage of global reserves. Some oil executives believe that recent seismic studies east of the Ural Mountains will prove that Russia possesses more oil and gas than today's most optimistic assessments. During the past three years—a time of decline in oil exports from countries not in the Organization of Petroleum Exporting Countries (OPEC)—60 percent of the growth in world oil exports has been in Russia (about 3 million barrels per day). The Russian wellhead price for crude oil is about $11 a barrel, and it is selling abroad for about $40.[11]

In addition, Russia's proven reserves of natural gas—natural gas is increasingly the modern world's fuel of choice—are the largest in the world and twice those of Iran, which possesses the second-largest reserves. Reserves today are listed as 1,680 trillion cubic feet with production at 21 trillion cubic feet and exports at 6.5 trillion cubic feet.[12] The wellhead price for Russian gas is approximately $10 per thousand cubic meters and it sells for $120–$130 in Western Europe.

Russia's current five-year economic boom has been fueled almost entirely by the expansion of the country's energy industry and the unusually high prices commanded for oil and gas on the world market. The energy industry accounts for about 20 percent of Russia's GDP, approximately 60 percent of its export revenues, and well over 40 percent of the government's fiscal revenue.[13] If world oil prices

---

9. "Russia Country Analysis," Energy Information Administration (EIA), U.S. Department of Energy (DOE), May 2004, www.eia.doe.gov/emeu/cabs/russia.html#oil.

10. Freedom of Information Agency, "Soviet Energy Data Resource Handbook" (SOV90-10021), May 1, 1990, p. 25. See www.foia.cia.gov; document in Special Collections.

11. Current Russian production figures do not include oil or gas from Kazakhstan, Azerbaijan, Turkmenistan, or Uzbekistan.

12. "Russia Country Analysis," EIA, DOE, May 2004, www.eia.doe.gov/emeu/cabs/russia.html#oil.

13. "Russia Country Analysis," EIA, DOE, May 2004, www.eia.doe.gov/emeu/cabs/russia.html.

Table 1.   Use of Russian Oil in Selected Countries of the Near Abroad

	Russian crude oil as a percentage of total crude oil consumption	Russian crude oil as a percentage of total crude oil imports
Ukraine[1] (2003)	61	86.6
Poland[2] (2002)	91	94.5
Estonia[3,4] (2001)	n.a.	n.a.
Latvia[3,4] (2001)	n.a.	n.a.
Lithuania[3] (2004)	90	100.0
Belarus (2004)	75	100.0

Sources:

Margarita Balmaceda, "EU Energy Policy and Future European Energy Markets," *Platts Oilgram News,* January 31, 2003.

"Poland's Oil Industry," *Poland Business Review,* according to preliminary figures presented by Poland's of Economy and Labor at a parliamentary committee in February 2003.

"Country Analysis: Baltic Sea Region" (Washington, D.C.: U.S. Department of Energy, Energy Information Administration, 2004), www.eia.doe.gov/emeu/cabs/baltics.html.

"Country Analysis: Ukraine" (Washington, D.C.: U.S. Department of Energy, Energy Information Administration, 2003), www.eia.doe.gov/emeu/cabs/ukraine.html.

"Energy Overview of the Republic of Estonia" (Washington, D.C.: U.S. Department of Energy, Fossil Energy Department, 2003), www.fe.doe.gov/international/CentralEastern%20Europe/estnover.html.

"Energy Overview of the Republic of Latvia" (Washington, D.C.: U.S. Department of Energy, Fossil Energy Department, 2003), www.fe.doe.gov/international/CentralEastern%20Europe/latvover.html.

"Ukrainian refineries short of oil because of new customs rules," Itar-Tass Weekly News, January 30, 2004.

Notes: Percentages are approximate.

1   Ukraine remains highly dependent on imported oil, most of which comes from Russia, with lesser amounts coming from Kazakhstan. In 2002, net oil imports totaled roughly 212,000 barrels per day, representing 70 percent of consumption

2   Approximately half of Poland's oil imports come from Russia; the United Kingdom, Iran, and Norway also supply significant amounts.

3   The countries of the Baltic region depend on Russia for approximately 90 percent of their oil supply.

4   Estonia and Latvia do not import or produce crude oil because of the lack of refining capacity in each country. Both nations serve as transshipment points for Russian oil and petroleum products and import all petroleum products used for consumption from sources that use 100 percent Russian crude oil. Although Estonia is not believed to have oil reserves, Latvia is estimated to have around 500 million barrels, although they remain untapped.

remain at or near $40–$45 per barrel for the next several years, it will fuel an impressive, if economically lopsided, growth in Russian GDP. President Putin has repeatedly warned that Russia's economy is overly dependent on energy exports, and one can assume that he is also concerned about the political power, especially abroad, of the energy elite. His government has done little, however, to encourage real diversification of Russia's economy. Oil and gas will remain Russia's only major source of export revenue. See tables 1, 2, and 3 for Russian energy exports to selected countries of the Near Abroad.[14]

Estimates show Russian crude oil output growing by an amount close to 10 million barrels per day by 2007 and from 10.4 to 12.0 million barrels per day by 2010. Exports are expected to increase to about 6 million barrels per day in 2007 and

---

14. "Near Abroad" refers to the former Soviet republics that had declared their independence by the time of the collapse of the Soviet Union in 1991.

Table 2.   Use of Russian Natural Gas in Selected Countries of the Near Abroad

	Annual imports from Russia (trillion cubic feet)	Annual imports from Russia (billion cubic meters)	Russian gas as a percentage of total gas consumption	Russian gas as a percentage of total gas imports
Ukraine (2001)	1.01	28.6	39	51
Poland[1,2] (2001)	0.26	7.4	58	84
Estonia[3,4] (2002)	0.02	0.7	100	100
Latvia[4] (2002)	0.05	1.4	88	100
Lithuania[4] (2002)	0.10	2.7	100	100
Belarus[5] (2002)	0.60	17.0	94	100

Sources:

"Country Analysis: Russia" (Washington, D.C.: U.S. Department of Energy, Energy Information Administration, 2004), www.eia.doe.gov/emeu/cabs/russia.html.

"Country Analysis: Baltic Sea Region" (Washington, D.C.: U.S. Department of Energy, Energy Information Administration, 2004), www.eia.doe.gov/emeu/cabs/baltics.html.

Margarita Balmaceda, "EU Energy Policy and Future European Energy Markets," *Platts Oilgram News*, January 31, 2003.

"The Resource Wealth Burden—Oil and Gas Sectors in the Former USSR," *OSW Report*, December 2003.

"Russian Gas Exports to Estonia Up 17 Pct in 2001," Baltic News Service, January 24, 2002.

Notes: Numbers and percentages are approximate.

1   On February 12, 2003, PGNiG and Gazprom renegotiated the original Yamal pipeline contract, reducing Poland's annual imports from Russia by one-third for the years 2003–2022.

2   Poland has an estimated 5.8 trillion cubic feet of natural gas reserves. In 2001, Poland produced 193 billion cubic feet, which met 39 percent of its domestic natural gas demand. Poland imports small amounts of natural gas from Germany and Norway.

3   Estonia has no natural gas reserves and therefore must import all of its natural gas for domestic consumption. Currently Estonia imports all of its supplies via the country's 250-mile pipeline network from Russia.

4   The countries of the Baltic region are entirely dependent on natural gas imports to meet their domestic consumption needs. The Baltic countries produced no natural gas in 2001 while they consumed a total of 202 billion cubic feet.

5   Belarus receives approximately 62 percent of its gas shipments from Gazprom and the remaining 38 percent from Itera (a Russian company closely linked to Gazprom leadership).

more than 7 million barrels per day in 2010.[15] Current figures, however, indicate that production and exports could reach these numbers before 2007 or 2010. LUKOIL, alone, is believed to have the largest reserves of oil and gas outside of the Persian Gulf states. Gazprom owns 66 percent of Russia's gas reserves, or 32 percent of the world's proven reserves, and produces 94 percent of Russia's natural gas, or 23 percent of the world's gas production. Gazprom accounts for 8 percent of Russian GDP and 25 percent of the federal government's tax receipts.[16]

---

15. Julian Lee, "Future Russian Oil Production: The CGES View" (London: Centre for Global Energy Studies, March 2004), www.cges.co.uk/pdf-lib/confpresentationJLCERIFSU.pdf.

Table 3. Use of Russian Electricity in Selected Countries of the Near Abroad

	Percentage of electricity consumed that is imported from Russia	Russian electricity as a percentage of total electricity imports
Ukraine (2002)	0.15	100.00
Poland[1,2] (2002)	4.64	13.75
Estonia[3,4] (2002)	N/A	N/A
Latvia[3,4] (2001)	19.04	11.09
Lithuania[3,4,5,6] (2003)	N/A	N/A
Belarus[5,6] (2003)	30.00	46.00

Sources:

"Country Analysis: Ukraine" (Washington, D.C.: U.S. Department of Energy, Energy Information Administration, 2003), www.eia.doe.gov/emeu/cabs/ukraine.html.

"Country Analysis: North Central Europe" (Washington, D.C.: U.S. Department of Energy, Energy Information Administration, 2003), www.eia.doe.gov/emeu/cabs/czech.html.

Anatoly Chubais, RAO-UES press conference, September 17, 2003, www.rao-ees.ru.

"Belarus Steps up Electricity Production in February," Itar-Tass, March 10, 2004.

"Country Analysis: Baltic Sea Region" (Washington, D.C.: U.S. Department of Energy, Energy Information Administration, 2004), www.eia.doe.gov/emeu/cabs/baltics.html.

Notes: Percentages are approximate.

1   The Polish power generation sector is the largest in Central and Eastern Europe. Poland is a net exporter of electricity.

2   In Poland, coal accounts for 97 percent of all electric power produced, with the remaining 3 percent coming from hydro-electric facilities.

3   Estonia and Lithuania are net electricity exporters, sending their surplus to neighboring Latvia and parts of northwest Russia. Energy imports from Russia are not consumed in either countries' electricity grids but allow for the reexport of Russian electricity to other markets. See "Country Analysis: Baltic Sea Region," www.eia.doe.gov/emeu/cabs/baltics.html.

4   When water levels in hydroelectric reservoirs are low, Latvia must import between 30 percent and 40 percent of its electricity. Latvia regularly imports electricity from Estonia and Lithuania in addition to what is imported from Russia.

5   Anatoly Chubais: "In Lithuania...we have taken over the export from Lithuania to Belarus. So, we supply energy to Belarus both from Russia and from Lithuania and we control this market," RAO-UES press conference, September 17, 2003.

6   In 2003, Belarus imported 7.6 billion kilowatt hours, 3.5 billion from Russia and 4.1 billion from Lithuania. Belarus halted electricity imports from Russia in February 2004 during a supply contract dispute although the contract was renewed in August.

Thus, it is hardly surprising that Russia's energy industry now receives a good deal of attention from outside observers. The surprise is that it did not receive even more critical analysis until the world became focused on Putin's destruction of YUKOS. The enormous economic clout of the Russian energy companies has translated into extraordinary domestic political influence by the owners and controllers of the industry whether or not the companies—such as Gazprom, which the state controls although it owns only 38 percent of the shares, and LUKOIL—are nominally privately owned. Russia's energy oligarchs played a decisive role in saving Boris Yeltsin in the presidential election of 1996, when the oligarchs—the group of seven—were able to combine their impressive financial resources in order to engineer the electoral defeat of Communist Party leader Gennady Zhuganov.

---

16. "Russia Country Analysis," EIA, DOE, May 2004, www.eia.doe.gov/emeu/cabs/russia.html#gas.

The oligarchs not involved with energy—Vladimir Gusinsky and Boris Bere-zovsky, for example, whose money came from investments in the media and large manufacturing plants—were exiled shortly after Putin became president in late 1999. The energy oligarchs, represented by Mikhail Friedman, Mikhail Khodor-kovsky, Vladimir Potanin, and Roman Abramovich, continued to exercise considerable political influence until the Russian government's campaigns against YUKOS and Mikhail Khodorkovsky commenced in the second half of 2003. Three of the four energy billionaires remain in control of their enormous energy assets and may have a respite from renationalization of their assets by virtue of the public relations drubbing the Putin government experienced when it moved against YUKOS. The international business community is convinced that the slow destruc-tion of YUKOS was a political reaction.

Control of Russia's energy resources and the right to develop and export them are the goals of intense competition by domestic clans, and, in several cases, by var-ious groups of former intelligence officers. The significant difference between the domestic prices of oil and gas in Russia and the current international price levels for oil and gas creates great pressure to export. Russian domestic oil is priced at less than one-quarter of the current (mid-2004) international level. While the price in Russia for natural gas is $28 per thousand cubic feet, it sells for an average of $80 per thousand cubic feet in Russia's Near Abroad, and at least $120–$130 per thou-sand cubic feet in Western Europe. The EU, in bilateral energy discussions and within the World Trade Organization (WTO) negotiations, has pressured Russia to bring its domestic prices closer to world market prices. The EU argues that low domestic prices give Russian industry a built-in competitive (presumably unfair) advantage over EU producers. Moscow argues that energy resources are the coun-try's natural competitive advantage and that it is politically unrealistic to expect Russia's relatively poor consumers to accept price levels anywhere near those found in the West. Russians argue, with some merit, that a rapid move to world pricing levels would be politically impossible for any country's leadership.

President Putin is well aware of the political power that he has as a result of Russia's energy resources. As such, he will not allow this sector to be controlled by private interests in Russia or by foreign energy corporations. His position on this issue sets the tone for Moscow's policies toward the West and in the Common-wealth of Independent States (CIS).

Power Projection in the Neighborhood

Russia is able to take advantage of other poor—but resource-rich—countries through energy pricing levels. Taking advantage of Turkmenistan's landlocked and politically isolated position, Russia was able to negotiate a 25-year agreement to take the major portion of Turkmen gas at $44 per thousand cubic meters (half to be paid in commodities) until 2006; the terms after 2007 have not been agreed upon although the volumes are expected to rise sharply to possibly 80 million cubic meters per year.[17] The gas from Turkmenistan will replace domestically produced gas in Russia, allowing Gazprom to meet its export commitments. This displaced

Russian gas will then be sold in Western markets by Gazprom for approximately three times as much per thousand cubic meters. Not a bad profit!

Turkmenistan had earlier hoped to gain Russian consent to construct its own gas pipelines through Russia. Although the Turkmen would have paid transit fees to Russia, they would have secured higher gas prices for themselves than they had from Moscow. At one point, Russia insisted that gas from Turkmenistan transported to Ukraine must be controlled by Itera, a spin-off of Gazprom's former management. Itera, of course, made a handy profit off the Turkmenistan-Ukraine connection. In late 2004, it appears that a new "daughter company" of Gazprom will be given the concession to supply Turkmen and some Russian gas to Ukraine.

These price differentials create enormous profit potential, particularly in an economy that is lacking in transparency and modern judicial and accounting systems. With much of the profit of Russian companies coming from international markets, there are unlimited opportunities for storing proceeds offshore where they can be used by energy company executives or by agencies of the Russian government. It is proving increasingly difficult to make a clear distinction between the two groups.

In dealing with Russian energy companies, the policies of President Putin's administration have done little to spur these companies to become more efficient. The government has also failed to increase internal competition by energy firms. Putin appears to share the widespread view in Russia that energy is too important a national asset to allow the market or any private individual free rein in deciding on issues such as links to foreign partners, pipeline construction, or competition for the right to explore new oil and gas fields. Putin and his advisers also share the view that members of the Russian energy industry should operate as an instrument of state policy rather than as autonomous international players, as is more common in the United States and parts of Europe.

Although Russia suffers from significant disadvantages owing to its enormous size, harsh climate, and shrinking population, its continental reach has endowed it with an enormous wealth of natural resources. Geography also favors Russia's ability to take economic advantage of its enormous oil and gas wealth. Most of the world's energy is consumed in the Northern Hemisphere, and the markets with the greatest need of additional energy supplies for the foreseeable future are in Europe, China, Japan, and the United States. In addition, many Asian suppliers, such as Kazakhstan and Turkmenistan, depend on the Russian pipeline system to market their own wealth.

With turmoil and instability in Iraq and much of the Middle East, the geographically closer Russian crude oil may in the future command a political premium in Europe as it competes against traditional oil producers in the Persian Gulf. The increasing use of natural gas, including liquefied natural gas (LNG), in the industrial world also favors Russia.

While today's Russia is hardly considered a bona fide democratic state, in most of the West the country is nonetheless seen as a more predictable and reliable energy trading partner than more troubled countries such as Saudi Arabia, Iraq,

17. "Russia Benefits from CIS Deals," *Petroleum Economist*, May 19, 2003, p. 30.

Iran, Venezuela, and Indonesia. Turmoil in the Middle East and the emergence of terrorism directed against the Saudi royal family has damaged the region's image as the one oil region to count on when the rest of the producing world is in trouble.

Russia's immense energy resources will only increase the country's influence in the coming years, as consuming nations scramble to line up secure sources of oil and gas imports. Japan and China are already assiduously courting the Kremlin to be the favored recipients of new East Siberian crude production. As North Sea production of oil and gas slumps, Europe may increasingly be competing with Japan and China for the same supplies. Furthermore, if political volatility in the Middle East continues, if Canada fails to find any large new deposits of light oil, and if Venezuela remains an uncertain supplier of crude to the United States, North America may find itself in sharp competition with Europe, China, and Japan for a share of Russia's additional production of both oil and gas.

The increased role of Russia as an incremental, and possibly sustainable, supplier of energy to the Northern Hemisphere will put the Russian government in a stronger position to resist pressure to conform to policies desired by the other Group of 8 (G-8) members.[18] This could potentially thwart U.S. and European efforts to prevent Russia from pursuing policies that endanger the political or economic sovereignty of countries in East Central Europe, the Caucasus, and Central Asia. Of course, either an unexpected breakthrough in finding alternative energy sources, or the collapse of world energy market prices through slower growth in the Chinese economy, or worldwide economic stagnation would reduce Russia's political bargaining power. The more likely scenario, however, is that Russian energy resources will be increasingly sought by the world's five largest economies—the United States, the EU, China, Japan, and India.

The Kremlin has, at times, considered creating a European energy cartel, modeled in a modest fashion after the highly successful OPEC. In the mid-1990s, Russia approached the Norwegians and suggested cooperating in the setting of gas export prices to Europe. The Norwegians declined the invitation, however. World energy specialists are now speculating that Russia by itself is attempting to gain control over Turkmenistan resources to set uniform gas export prices. Domination by Russia would prevent it from being a cartel in the classic sense.

---

18. The Group of 8 comprises Canada, France, Germany, Italy, Japan, Russia, the United Kingdom, and the United States.

Government–Energy Company Ties in Russia

Profit Maximization Challenged by State Policy

With Russia significantly weakened as a military and ideological power, its nostalgia for past imperial glory is likely to be reflected in its international trade policy. Even during the Soviet period, international trade was closely tied to foreign policy. Furthermore, implementation of this strategy was often in the hands of the intelligence agencies, which generally handled cash transactions outside of Russia. The Ministry of Foreign Affairs and the Ministry of Economic Development and Trade often took a back seat to the KGB and GRU on foreign commercial issues.[19]

Since the end of the Cold War, Russians have realized that possession of atomic weapons confers only limited status in a world where nuclear proliferation is so prevalent that even a fifth-rate power such as North Korea can threaten the world with nuclear weapons. Therefore, Russia's power elite recognize that the country's strongest instrument for influencing foreign events is the energy card—Russia's massive reserves of oil, gas, and electricity. In the 1980s, the Soviet Union, which then controlled the Caspian region, was the largest producer of oil, gas, and electricity in the world.

Moscow has announced plans to return to the impressive production levels of the 1980s within the boundaries of present-day Russia and to use the resulting export revenue to raise living standards at home to levels closer to those in Western Europe. With less publicity, the Kremlin and the "power ministries"—Ministry of Foreign Affairs, Ministry of Defense, Ministry of the Interior, and intelligence organizations—plan to use this energy wealth to increase Russia's leverage in international security affairs and influence the political and economic policies of Russia's trading partners.

This leverage, of course, has the greatest effect in those countries that depend almost entirely on Russia for supplies of oil or natural gas, or both. Thus, the most vulnerable are those in the relatively poor Near Abroad countries that have neither the wealth nor the geographic location that would allow them to diversify their energy imports. Possession of large quantities of surplus oil and gas provides a dangerous advantage to those countries, like Russia, willing to use this power in ways

---

19. The KGB (*Komitet Gosudarstvennoy Bezopasnosti,* or Committee for State Security) existed as the USSR's internal and external intelligence service until eventually becoming the FSB (*Federalnaya Sluzhba Bezopasnosti,* or Federal Security Service) in 1995. GRU is an acronym for the Soviet Union's military intelligence organization.

that corrupt and weaken already poor neighbors that have not had time to build strong, transparent governmental institutions.

The problem of energy corruption in the region is not entirely Russia's fault, but lack of reform in Russia greatly exacerbates and reinforces corruption in the entire area. In Transparency International's 2004 report on global corruption, Russia tied Mozambique for 86th place out of 133 countries.[20]

Still to be resolved is the question of whether the primary function of energy firms should be to maximize profits for their shareholders or for the state and Russia's citizens. Because Russia has a president who was formerly a KBG officer and a prime minister who has an intelligence service background, it is not surprising that the pendulum in Russia has now shifted to using the energy companies as instruments of state policy. A main goal and priority of the Putin government's energy strategy until 2020 is to use Russia's substantial energy resources and strong fuel-energy industry as a base for expanding Russian political power. In addition, the government's white paper on the subject of energy recognizes that the country's geopolitical influence will depend on its strong position in world energy markets.[21] Although this goal may not conform to statements by Putin that Russia must diversify and get away free itself from a heavy dependence on energy production and exports, a shift away from energy revenue does not appear likely before 2020.

Russia's major energy companies are often asked forced to export their products through Russian ports, and thereby forgo higher profits in the short and medium term, in order to weaken any potential political or financial leverage over Russia by the country's neighbors. For example, the construction of the giant Baltic Pipeline System (BPS), which carries oil to the port of Primorsk, is designed to handle 60 million tons of oil annually by the end of 2005. This huge and expensive complex is being built, in part, to avoid relying on oil transit through the three Baltic states. All three Baltic states now have underused oil export capacity and, consequently,

Selected Russian Crude Oil Export Pipelines

Source: U.S. Department of Energy, Energy Information Administration.

the ability to increase exports cheaply. The BPS is designed specifically to bypass the Baltic states by directing most West Siberian crude and southern Ural production to a Russian-controlled port.

The Russian government is also encouraging Gazprom to build an undersea gas pipeline from Russia to Germany, thereby bypassing Poland and Belarus, even though the cost of construction will be three to four times as much as running a

---

20. *Global Corruption Report 2004* (Berlin: Transparency International, 2004), 246, www.globalcorruptionreport.org/.

21. Ministry of Industry and Energy of Russia, "Energeticheskaia strategiia Rossii na period do 2020 goda, utverzhdena racporiazheniem Pravitel′stva Rossiiskoi Federatsii ot 28 avgusta 2003 g. No 1234-p," www.mte.gov.ru/docs/32/103.html.

parallel pipe along the Yamal I route through Poland. At the same time, the Kremlin is doing everything possible to block pipelines that would bypass Russia in sending Caspian crude to Central and Western Europe. The Kremlin has a sophisticated policy of becoming increasingly independent of other countries while simultaneously creating dependence on Russian energy in those same countries. Unless Russian exports become more diversified, however, the increased energy exports can create a fiscal dependence within Russia.

Russia and Iraq

Although Russia's close ties to the Saddam Hussein regime in Iraq are not news, information released by the new Iraq authorities confirms that energy companies with extremely close ties to the Kremlin were operating during the past few years as direct instruments of Russian state foreign policy in contravention of the Kremlin's commitments to the UN.

After the U.S. invasion of Iraq in 2003, when coalition forces and Iraqi officials started sorting through the mountain of documents in Saddam Hussein's Ministry of Oil they discovered that the Iraqi government was exploiting the UN-operated oil-for-food program in order to illegally reward Iraq's friends. The international press reported extensively in early 2004 that UN controls were subverted to reward companies, individual organizations, foreign officials, and even churches for their support of Saddam Hussein's government. It came as no great surprise that the largest beneficiaries were Russian energy companies. Even Russia's Orthodox Church was listed as a recipient of financial benefits. The UN is conducting an internal investigation of the payments, but the evidence at this point indicates that Russia gained far more than any other country from Saddam's goodwill.

According to a January 2004 article in the Baghdad-based newspaper, al-Mada, by far the largest beneficiary was the Russian state, which reportedly was allocated 1,366,000,000 barrels of oil. President Putin's Unity Party was slated to get 34 million barrels. Other reports state that individuals in the office of President Putin were to receive 92 million barrels. Zarubezhneft—a Russian state-owned company whose management reports directly to the Kremlin is generally unknown in the West—was listed as having received or being slated to receive (it is unclear at this point how much they actually benefited before the invasion of Iraq) 174.5 million barrels of oil. Industry analysts estimate that the profit to the company was at least 50¢ on each barrel.[22] The second-largest recipient was Rosneft, earmarked to receive 66.9 million barrels; LUKOIL was listed for 63 million barrels. The Moscow Oil Company was listed at 25.1 million barrels. Gazprom was down for 26 million barrels, and Soyusneftgaz for 25.5 million. Transneft was to receive (or received) 9 million barrels. The more-transparent YUKOS was to receive only 2 million barrels.[23]

---

22. 100 cents (¢) equal 1 U.S. dollar.

23. All numbers are from "The Beneficiaries of Saddam's Oil Vouchers," Al-Mada, January 25, 2004 (translated by the Middle East Media Research Institute, www.memri.org).

The Russian Orthodox Church was slated to receive 5 million barrels. The church, like most of the other alleged recipients, denies deriving any benefits from the Iraqi government, but the church was a supporter of Saddam Hussein right up to the invasion by coalition forces.

Privatization and Pseudoprivatization

Zarubezhneft is one of the most opaque of Russia's energy companies.[24] Its officials report directly to the Russian Presidential Administration (PA), led by Alexander Voloshin, who was chief of the PA until November 2003. The company has several members of the *siloviki*[25] in top management positions. Zarubezhneft publishes little information on its domestic or foreign operations except that it acknowledges being involved in energy projects in South Africa, Sudan, Vietnam, and Iran.

The present head of Zarubezhneft is Nikolai Tokarev, former vice president of Transneft.[26] Tokarev is reportedly a former deputy head of the current Russian Federal Security Service (FSB) and Putin ally.[27] Zarubezhneft and Transneft have close ties to the security services. Transneft's board contains several former KGB officers. Western analysts assume that executives of Russia's intelligence organizations and power ministries share the opinion that national interests are promoted most effectively by operating covertly with the traditional tools of subversion, disinformation, and bribery. The power of this group was weakened under Gorbachev, used only marginally by Yeltsin, and is now reasserting its influence under former KGB officer Putin.

Although Rosneft is more forthcoming with basic information on its operations, like Zarubezhneft and Transneft, the company has close ties to former KGB and FSB officers in St. Petersburg. In fact, influential Russians often refer to Rosneft as "the KGB company." Rosneft's new chief executive officer is Igor Sechin, a former KGB officer, who until mid-2004 worked in the PA. Rosneft may have played a role in the destruction of YUKOS as an independent energy company (see page 21), especially as the announced merger with Gazprom becomes a reality.[28]

Western energy executives who have negotiated with Russia's major energy companies report that any major deal with a Western firm or an investment in another country must be approved by the PA, if not personally by President Putin.

---

24. Established in 1967 as a foreign economic cooperation association within the USSR's Ministry of Oil Industry, Zarubezhneft was preserved by a presidential decree in 1995 attaching it to the Ministry of Industry and Energy. On a self-sustaining basis (contributing more than $0.5 billion to the state each year), the company is tasked with implementing cooperation between Russian and foreign companies and organizations in developing the energy industry within Russia and abroad. President Putin by official decree called for the transformation of Zarubezhneft into a public joint stock company in 2004; 100 percent of the shares are to be retained by the state.

25. *Siloviki* are former intelligence officers who hold responsible positions in the Putin government.

26. By government decree in 1992, the Central Department for Oil Transportation and Supplies (Glavtransneft) became the legal entity Transneft. The company continues to be 100 percent state owned, and it operates as the state's oil transportation monopoly.

27. "Russia Forges Ties with Iran, Iraq," *Energy Compass*, October 5, 2001.

Because many top officials in the PA are former intelligence officers, one should presume that this group has a voice in any strategic investment by a Western company.

The two largest Russian companies, Gazprom and Transneft, are operated as government-run monopolies and will remain so for the foreseeable future. Although LUKOIL[29] and Rosneft are allegedly privately owned, independent companies, they behave as state-owned enterprises rather than commercial enterprises. Transneft is the company of first choice when the Kremlin wants to enforce its energy policy abroad.

The political power of Gazprom was starkly demonstrated in 2000, when Putin forced oligarch Vladimir Gusinsky to divest all his media stock in Russia in order to avoid prison and seizure of all his assets. In a surprise move, Putin required Gusinsky to turn his complete interest in Media-Most (his giant media company) over to Gazprom, which then created Gazprom-Media. Putin's influence with Gazprom was sufficient to ensure that the media company would in the future be a docile instrument of the government. On June 1, 2004, Leonid Parfyonov, a popular commentator on one of Gazprom's television stations, was fired for protesting state censorship of the media, demonstrating again the close ties between Gazprom and the political interests of the Kremlin.[30] Putin may have chosen Gazprom at least in part because of its reputation of being a home for ex-KGB officers.

Khodorkovsky, Friedman, and Abramovich had talked openly about competing with Transneft in building export pipelines, particularly one from western Siberia to Murmansk. In a speech in Murmansk, Prime Minister Mikhail Kasyanov quickly shot down this plan as well as hopes for any private pipelines when he said that Russian pipelines should belong to the state.[31] Any talk about private pipeline construction has halted since the legal-political move to bring down YUKOS. Kasyanov's successor, Mikhail Fradkov reasserted this view in April when he remarked, "There will be no private pipelines in Russia. This is our infrastructure and competitive advantage and it is necessary [for the state] to control it."[32]

Before the jailing of Khodorkovsky, there had been some degree of competition abroad between LUKOIL, TNK, and YUKOS for the purchase of foreign facilities and to dominate the retail business in neighboring countries. LUKOIL was generally stronger in the northern part of Europe (with the exception of Lithuania), whereas YUKOS and TNK concentrated on southern Europe (with the exception of Ukraine). Until recently a degree of competition existed between Gazprom and

---

28. Rosneft (Rossiskaya neft´) was established in 1995 by a decree of the government of the Russian Federation. Rosneft included the remaining state-owned oil and gas production enterprises, oil refineries, and distribution companies. Although the firm continues to be entirely state owned, in September 2004 it was announced that Rosneft will be integrated into Gazprom and become a subsidiary.

29. LUKOIL was formed as a state-owned oil concern in late 1991 by a Soviet Council of Ministers resolution uniting three oil-producing enterprises and three processing enterprises under the LangepasUraiKogalymneft name.

30. Susan B. Glasser, "Russian TV Host Dismissed," *Washington Post*, June 3, 2004, p. A16.

31. Sabrine Tavernise, "Russians Ponder Two Competing Oil Routes in East Asia," *New York Times*, January 14, 2003, p. W1.

32. "There Will Be No Private Pipelines in Russia," *Russian Oil and Gas Report*, April 14, 2004.

Itera (nominally a U.S.-based company but in fact a spin-off of Gazprom). Itera tended to hold positions in markets where Gazprom was not interested in making large investments or until the Russian Ministry of Industry and Energy decides that Russia should have a larger, more powerful company in place that can more effectively represent state interests. Itera, which was established in part to provide profit to the Yeltsin family and its friends, has now seen some of its assets taken away and returned to Gazprom, but in some countries Itera continues to serve the interests of the Russian state. Ukraine and Latvia have seen a host of other Gazprom spin-offs set up for political reasons.

It is usually impossible to separate the commercial activities of Transneft, Gazprom, and LUKOIL from Russia's foreign policy objectives. In the United States and Western Europe, only the most politically sensitive investment decisions would be subject to veto by the top political figure. Roland Nash, head of research at Renaissance Capital, a Moscow investment bank, has stated, "In the non-resource sector, the state is quite happy to let the free market generate growth and diversification, but it seems clear that Mr. Putin wants to call the shots in the natural resource sector."[33]

Khodorkovsky and the Fall of YUKOS

The strongest energy competitor within Russia has been YUKOS, which transformed itself into the country's most Westernized and transparent firm. Its willingness to open its books to public scrutiny and hire U.S. and European managers and consultants engendered a fair degree of respect in Western financial markets and by governments of East Central Europe. Such transparency was especially important to those governments that were trying to prevent the takeover of their energy industry by firms that were more willing instruments of Russian foreign policies.

As YUKOS became increasingly transparent, transforming itself into a company designed to maximize profit, it became more vulnerable to attack by other members of the Russian establishment who were jealous of its independence and soaring profits. One well-connected Russian observer claimed that the Rosneft/Meshprombank group in St. Petersburg, which is considered representative of the intelligence community, had helped initiate the downfall of Khodorkovsky in order to seize some of YUKOS's assets and prevent the company from becoming the dominant Russian player in Western Europe and the United States. The naming of Igor Sechin to be Rosneft's chief executive and the increasing influence of Rosneft within the Kremlin appear to confirm that speculation.

Paul Klebnikov, editor of *Forbes Russia* who was assassinated outside his office in July 2004, asked his readers to compare Sibneft[34] and YUKOS. In his last interview, he stated, "On all charges that were made against YUKOS—non-payment of taxes, non-patriotism and political interests—Sibneft is much worse than YUKOS.

---

33. Andrew Jack, "An Assertive Kremlin Puts Oil Investigators on Eggshells," *Financial Times*, June 1, 2004, sec. 1, p. 18.

However, Sibneft flourishes and is being patronized by the Kremlin, while YUKOS is being dismembered."[35] Klebnikov noted that Roman Abramovich, head of Sibneft, is a friend of Putin while Khodorkovsky is an independent person, and friends of the president tend to receive preferential treatment: "But if you apply the law so strictly to one oligarch why do not do the same with respect to another one who violated the law and public morale more severely?"[36] It is becoming more evident that YUKOS is being dismantled as part of a policy to increase the state's control over the foreign operations of Russian energy companies.

The move by the Putin government against YUKOS chief, Mikhail Khodorkovsky, and the financial weakening of the company has already reversed the earlier trend toward greater transparency in Russian energy companies. Although there are many reasons for Putin's move against YUKOS, many of Khodorkovsky's problems started after he opened the company's books and all YUKOS's chief executives and board members declared their personal net worth. Khodorkovsky's declaration of $7 billion did not endear him to the executives of Transneft, LUKOIL, and Gazprom, who have avoided the semitransparent policies of YUKOS.

The arrest and jailing of Khodorkovsky elicited a chorus of protests from U.S. and European leaders and from Western shareholders who had been encouraged by the Putin administration to invest in Russian companies. Nevertheless, complaints by Western leaders have had little effect on the presidential administration, the power ministries, and rival company leaders as they steadily chip away at YUKOS's control of its assets. Yulia Latynina, writing in the *St. Petersburg Times*, stated, "the YUKOS affair made clear what happens to companies that want to be transparent. The more transparent they become, the less they depend on the Kremlin. The drive for transparency is equated with a revolt against the regime. The Russian businessmen are no fools. They've learned their lesson."[37]

The Kremlin appears to have decided that it can no longer trust oil executives who are considered members of the Yeltsin-era oligarchy unless they are part of companies like LUKOIL, which have demonstrated a willingness to follow the lead of the Kremlin. These companies want to replace executives with people whose first loyalties are to the Russian state rather than to their private shareholders.

British Petroleum's (BP) $7 billion investment in TNK[38] in 2003 may, as BP hopes, end up changing the culture of the Russian-dominated partnership, but the jury is still out as to whether the Western partner can pull off the change. BP, which had its assets illegally stripped in the mid-1990s by the same people now listed as

---

34. In 1995 the Russian government, by decree of President Boris Yeltsin, combined a production entity, an exploration branch, a marketing company, and the Omsk refinery into Sibneft (Siberian Oil). Managed under the Loans for Shares program since its inception, the company became privately owned after going through a series of auctions beginning in 1996 in which the state sold 49 percent of Sibneft shares. The government's remaining 51 percent was then purchased in 1997 by Financial Petroleum Corporation, which quickly moved to consolidate Sibneft holdings into a unified share.

35. "The Last Interview of Paul Klebnikov," *Izvestia*, July 12, 2004.

36. Ibid.

37. Yulia Latynina, "Oligarchs Trade Davos Forum for Courcheval Frolic," *St. Petersburg Times*, February 3, 2004.

partners in the TNK-BP venture, is already supporting TNK investment decisions abroad that are opposed by both the EU and the United States. The most obvious example of this is BP's new opposition to the development of the Odessa-Brody pipeline project, which would transport Caspian crude to Western markets. The Russian government strongly opposes the project because it bypasses Russia and would give more energy independence to both Caspian producers and European consumers. BP, because of its relationship with TNK, ended up on the side of Putin and greater Russian control over oil transportation routes.

The complicated relationship between Russia's energy companies, the Kremlin administration, and the more narrow interests of the country's intelligence community appears to have become even more opaque in the past year. One small positive sign on the horizon is Russia's agreement in principle with the EU over membership in the WTO. While membership is still in the distant future for Russia, an enforceable agreement with the EU could bring a modest degree of transparency to the activities of Russia's energy companies as they continue to gain control over the energy infrastructure in East Central Europe.

During the post-Soviet period, some former leaders of Communist parties and executives of major industries in East Central Europe have benefited economically far beyond their dreams during the previous decade. They were able to seize much of the region's wealth by taking advantage of their personal ties to other national leaders and their access to Communist Party funds and displaying a general lack of moral scruples. The sole exception to this occurred in Estonia, where a new generation of younger, inexperienced leaders was able to wrest power from the former Communist elite in the immediate post-Communist period of 1991 to 1993. An open economy with close ties to the Nordic region was quickly established before the remaining Estonian-Russian *nomenklatura*[39] could organize themselves and develop business partnerships with their contacts in Russia. Estonia's laissez-faire policies quickly opened the country to Western investors, which helped block some of the money-making schemes of the former elite who so skillfully maneuvered for control in Ukraine, Latvia, and Lithuania. Members of the former power elite in these countries continued to cultivate personal ties with former party and economic leaders in Moscow. In Poland, the situation was mixed, with only a few members of the former elite profiting from their ties with Russia.

After an initial hesitation in the early 1990s, these former Communist leaders began to recognize that they had a priceless advantage over the budding entrepreneurial class in Eastern Europe. They could capitalize on their well-established personal relationships with members of the former *nomenklatura* in Russia. It is no

38. TNK (Tyumen Neftyanaya Kompaniya, or Tyumen Oil Company) was formed in 1995 as a state-owned oil company. A series of auctions between 1997 and 1999 allowed the consortium of the Alfa Group and the Access/Renova Group to gain complete control of the company. In 2003, TNK merged with the majority of British Petroleum's Russian assets and formed TNK-BP, with each company maintaining a 50 percent stake in the venture.
39. The *nomenklatura* consists of former high-ranking members of the past Communist system who held positions of high responsibility in industry and government. During the time of the Soviet Union, they existed as a small elite, and they have since translated their former authority on modern terms.

coincidence that these ex-officials focused on acquiring wealth through access to energy resources. When asked why he targeted banks, the famous U.S. bank robber Willie Sutton, answered, "Because that's where the money is." Likewise, energy industries are potentially the wealthiest sector in Russia and that's where the money is. Former officials of Communist East Central Europe played the roles of facilitators and, in many cases, owners of companies set up to import and distribute Russia's energy wealth.

The *Siloviki* in the Russian Energy Industry

Novaya Gazeta estimates that there are currently more than 6,000 former intelligence officers who hold office in responsible positions in the present Russian government.[40] Vladimir Putin is the best known of this group. Others include Premier Mikhail Y. Fradkov, relatively new to his job, who also reportedly served as an intelligence officer overseas.[41] These individuals are popularly categorized in Russia as *siloviki*. According to Olga Kryshtanovskaya, a leading Russian sociologist, the proportion of *siloviki* in the highest levels of Kremlin power has increased from 4.8 percent under Mikhail Gorbachev to 58.3 percent under Vladimir Putin.[42] Some of these people are considered modernists in that they want Russia to westernize its economy and strengthen its ties to the rest of the world. The *siloviki* are often well educated, speak foreign languages, and have traveled extensively abroad. Most of this group, however, appears to share the traditional view that Russia is surrounded by hostile forces and that international relations are a zero-sum struggle. This may be a somewhat oversimplified view of such a large group of individuals, but no reliable scholarly study about their views on public policy issues has been published.

Significant implications arise from the growing power of former and present intelligence officers. It is worth recalling Putin's remark that "there cannot be former KGB officers," implying that the KGB mind-set continues after leaving the service.[43] One can reasonably assume that this group is almost uniformly angered over the breakup of the Soviet Union and the weakening of Russian state power. Certainly their own influence and that of their organization were diminished significantly by former president Boris Yeltsin's acceptance of independence by the 14 non-Russian republics and by the withdrawal of Russian troops from the former Warsaw Pact states.

Restored to power, the *siloviki* are wedded to the concept of a strong Russian state—one where federalism is weakly practiced and all elements of society, including the business sector, are first and foremost instruments of state power. Trained in clandestine operations and with career experience in one of the world's least transparent organizations, the *siloviki* are generally ill equipped to operate in an open society of checks and balances and where a greater degree of transparency is

---

40. "Chekists in the Corridors of Power," *Novaya Gazeta*, July 2003, no. 50.
41. "West Watches Nervously as the Kremlin Raises Its Flags," *Financial Times*, March 3, 2004.
42. "Russia Still Has the Attributes of a Democracy, but, Managed by the *Siloviki*, This Could Become Illusory," *Financial Times*, February 24, 2004, Section: Comments & Analysis.
43. "Dangerous People in Civilian Clothing," *Yezhenedelnyi Zhurnal*, March 15, 2004, p. 21.

required for a successful business career. Equally important, these officials and their predecessors have little faith in negotiations that are designed to produce solid and long-lasting benefits to both sides. The zero-sum mentality prevalent in the intelligence or police world does not readily translate into the world of business—particularly the world of international trade between democratic nations, where a win-win strategy is the desired norm.

During the chaotic early years of the Yeltsin government, several thousand former intelligence officers were formally released from service or were kept in their jobs but paid only sporadically. The greatest demand for their services in the early 1990s was by companies that had acquired control, in some cases legally but in most instances illegally, over former state assets. The assets with the greatest potential for instant wealth were Russia's natural resources, with oil and natural gas deposits and facilities being the most attractive.

It is no surprise, therefore, that several hundred experienced former intelligence officers were drawn to work for Russia's oil pipeline monopoly Transneft, while others signed on with the natural gas monopoly Gazprom, and still others became important figures in the country's state oil companies or in newly privatized companies such as LUKOIL, Rosneft, TNK, YUKOS, or Sibneft. The skill sets required of these people in the early Wild West days of asset acquisition were often criminal in nature, with the struggle over property often resolved violently. Every company needed a *krisha* or "roof"—a strong, politically connected security organization to protect it from powerful rivals. Although many former officers of the KGB or GRU had ethical objections to the scramble to seize assets belonging to the Russian people, the early 1990s was a period of survival of the fittest, and those with families to support or criminal tendencies could always rationalize their participation in the rampant corruption that characterized those years.

Gradually, many *siloviki* picked up enough knowledge of the shady sides of internal business to become useful in moving profits abroad and helping to avoid state intervention by tax authorities and labor inspectors. Today, though, all of the major energy companies have intelligence-service veterans in high-level positions, with Transneft, Gazprom, LUKOIL, and Rosneft home to the largest number of *siloviki*. According to the *Moscow Times*, state-owned enterprises are funding sources for much of the *siloviki*, with Gazprom and Rosneft particularly important.[44] Some Russians even speak of Rosneft as "the KGB company."

Although no evidence directly links Transneft chief Simyon Weinshtok to the KGB, his vice president, Sergei Grigoriev, is unquestionably a former KGB officer.[45] Transneft's new vice-president is Yevgeni Shkolov, who worked with President Putin in St. Petersburg as a KGB officer.[46] The September 2004 announcement by Putin that Gazprom and Rosneft would be merged in order to help attract foreign

44. Anatoly Medetsky, "Dissecting Siloviki's Pyramid of Power," *Moscow Times*, December 24, 2003, p. A1.

45. "Kak Vainshtok Putina Perekhitral," *Russkii Fokus*, March 9, 2003, http://scandaly.ru/news/news1496.html.

46. Vladimir Rakhman′kov, "Evgenii Shkolov stal pomoshchnikom Aleksandra Voloshina," *Kursiv*, October 9, 2002, www.cursiv.ru/articles/issue.php?id=340.

investment may be true. Nevertheless, one can count on the foreign owners having little control of the company's direction. The *siloviki* will still call the shots.

KGB officers became key facilitators in preparing deals with foreign business partners, particularly in the early 1990s. Cash transactions with individuals and entities abroad were always handled by the KGB. Generally, these arrangements were with their most unscrupulous counterparts in the rest of the former Soviet Union or in Warsaw Pact countries. In the brave new world of post-Soviet Russia, an individual with a network of personal contacts, toughness (or ruthlessness), and an understanding of the mechanics of Russian society is invaluable.

In addition, it helped to have someone with access to derogatory information on political or business opponents along with knowledge of how to develop information on an individual that could be used to influence that person's business decisions. One Polish intelligence official complained that with so many former Russian intelligence personnel present during energy negotiations with Polish companies, it is difficult to know who is or is not still on active duty.

Unfortunately for the evolution of business transparency, Russia's most famous member of the *siloviki* is the country's current president, and his use of nondemocratic methods to deal with political opposition only reinforces the negative behavior of Russian companies operating abroad. The Kremlin's campaign to recapture control of YUKOS, which had become Russia's most transparent energy company, only strengthens suspicion abroad that Putin is determined to make Russia's energy companies—whether oil, gas, or electricity—first and foremost instruments of state security policy. The nascent idea that they should be autonomous players pursuing profit maximization has suffered a serious setback in Russia.

Price of Small-Country Energy Dependence

Supply Dependence

Energy dependence in and of itself does not pose a serious threat to a country's political or security system. The United States, Western Europe, and, to an increasing extent, China are highly dependent on imports of oil and gas. The United States imports 62 percent of its oil for consumption.[47] This dependence may not be an intelligent use of the country's financial resources, but by itself it has little effect on government transparency. This type of dependence on one particular foreign source of energy does not automatically result in the ability of another government to significantly influence foreign or security policy in that country's favor. Saudi Arabia's influence in the United States is not inconsequential, and yet U.S. policy toward the Israel-Palestine dispute does not appear to have been significantly influenced by Riyadh's deep unhappiness with Washington's tilt toward Israel.

The key to limiting an energy supplier's influence is the recipient country's ability to diversify its sources of energy imports. This requires an open and transparent business climate, sufficient wealth to pay for higher-priced imports in times of crisis, sufficient storage capacity, and, to some degree, a favorable geographic position that is open to international trade routes. Unfortunately, Estonia, Latvia, Lithuania, Poland, and Ukraine have neither the financial resources nor the geographical benefit of having more than one reasonably priced energy supplier (Russia in this case) close at hand. Alternative suppliers of energy, such as Norway, even if their transportation costs are not significantly higher than Russia's, are not disposed to offer significant price breaks on oil and gas exports to countries not financially able to pay world market prices.

In varying degrees, all five of these countries became locked into a Moscow-directed energy supply network during the 70 years of the Soviet Union's existence. The cause was not only Soviet imperialism, but also a flawed attempt to promote efficiency in the transportation of natural resources. The autarkic economic policies of the Soviet leadership, therefore, left those who quit the empire in 1990–1991 with fewer import options. Although all five countries depend on Russia for large segments of their energy needs, the circumstances in each country differ greatly. Large coal deposits in Poland, deep veins of oil shale in Estonia, and two nuclear power reactors in Lithuania have given each country a measure of independence,

---

47. "United States Country Analysis Brief," EIA, DOE, April 2004, www.eia.doe.gov/emeu/cabs/usa.html.

but a high degree of dependence on Russian energy resources still exists. Although Poland's coal production has allowed the country to produce a small surplus of electricity generation, it still relies on Russia for about 91 percent of all oil used for domestic consumption and almost 60 percent of its natural gas use.

It is a historic irony that EU membership will likely make Poland more, rather than less, dependent on Russian energy imports. Because adherence to the goals of the Kyoto Treaty and to the EU's environmental rules is not optional for EU members, Poland will likely be forced to close down much of its coal production and substitute natural gas for power generation. With Gazprom the effective monopoly supplier of gas to Poland, Moscow's leverage with Warsaw will probably increase, at least in the energy area.

The situation in the Baltic states and Ukraine presents a different environment for Russian energy than does Poland. Never having been part of the Soviet Union provides the Poles with a more independent mind-set as they deal with the Russians. In addition, while Russia would not hesitate to cut off energy to the Baltic states, the Kremlin would be reluctant to target Poland for a supply disruption. Geography and size make Poland too important for that tactic, and any hostile action against that country would negatively affect Russia's relations with Germany.

EU membership is having a similar effect on Lithuania. Under strong pressure from the EU, Vilnius has agreed (at least for now) to close both of its relatively modern, but Soviet-designed, nuclear power reactors. Like Poland, Lithuania has been able to produce all of its electricity needs, with some remaining to export to Latvia and Belarus. Conversely, almost 100 percent of Lithuania's oil and natural gas is imported from Russia, and Lithuania is totally dependent on Russia's nuclear-fuel industries for reactor fuel rods.

Latvia's domestic production of electricity from hydroelectric plants accounts for approximately half of its needs, and it imports most of the rest from Lithuania and Estonia. Like Lithuania, however, Latvia depends on Russia for 85 percent of its natural gas imports and 100 percent of its crude oil supplies. Latvia's oil products, which come from Estonia and Lithuania, must be refined at the Russian-controlled facility at Mazeikiai, with the crude supply originating in Russia.

Estonia's oil shale, produced in the area of its eastern border with Russia, may give the country a temporary surplus of electricity generation, but, here again, EU environmental rules may well force Estonia to reduce its production of oil slate and substitute Russian natural gas or oil for at least part of its power production. Estonia has been a leader in putting together a project that will link the Baltic and Nordic states with a 315-megawatt underwater cable. The plan, know as Estlink, is designed to shelter the three Baltic states from greater dependence on Russia for their electricity needs. The project was adopted by Finland and the three Baltic states in July 2004, but it will be several years before Finnish electricity exports play a role in Baltic consumption patterns. Of course, electricity that would be imported from Finland might, in turn, be dependent on Russian natural gas shipments to Finland, although the planned construction of a third Finnish nuclear power plant may reduce this dependence. Together with Finnish imports, a substantial life extension of Lithuania's Ignalina II nuclear power station or the construction of a new nuclear plant in Lithuania would provide a greater degree of independence in electricity consumption.

Estonia was the quickest to lessen its dependence on Russia. Its trade with Russia decreased from 57 percent of exports and 46 percent of imports in 1991 to 21 percent of exports and 28 percent of imports in 1992. By 2002, Russia accounted for no more than 9 percent of Estonia's imports and 4 percent of exports.[48] In 1995, the Russian ambassador to Estonia admitted to this author that Moscow's trade policies, including the use of energy interruptions, had backfired. He complained that he was unable to convince the Foreign Ministry in Moscow of the shortsightedness of its trade restrictions and its threats of retaliation for Estonia's cooperation with NATO. Russian economic pressure has often, at least in the short run, actually decreased Moscow's leverage over countries like Estonia in the military and non-energy trade areas.

Ukraine's size (as the second largest European country after Russia) and its proximity to Russia place it in an atypical position. Despite its four operating nuclear power plants, it is the only one of the five states that depends on Russia for most of its electricity needs (70 percent). Ukraine, along with Germany, is one of the world's largest importers of Russian natural gas. Even so, it imports directly from Russia only 40 percent of its natural gas consumption. The remainder is produced domestically or is imported from Turkmenistan.

In Ukraine, LUKOIL has managed to gain 100 percent ownership of the Odessa refinery and 50 percent of the ZAO large chemical and petrochemical complex,[49] and, of course, it owns 100 percent of LUKOIL Ukraine, which has 185 gasoline stations. Ukrainian energy specialists believe that, although LUKOIL has other substantial investments in Ukraine, the firm prefers to use less transparent ownership titles to obscure its large presence. President Kuchma and members of his family have close personal ties to LUKOIL and may have shares in some of the company's investments in Ukraine, including the Odessa refinery. In June 2003, a *Pravda* article stated:

> It took the Russian oil industry eight years to change the situation in Ukraine fundamentally. The national fuel business of Ukraine is already living in compliance with the law that is determined by Russian companies. However, bigger changes are about to unfold. Russian oligarchs are trying to gain total control over the oil industry and the oil export infrastructure in Ukraine. The consequences of such changes for Ukraine are already obvious: the country may be deprived of its economic independence.[50]

On August 18, 2004, Putin and Kuchma signed a 15-year agreement on oil transit that will result in Ukraine being even more dependent on Russia for future oil supplies and for the domestic construction of additional pipeline capacity.[51] Under

48. "How Russia Lost Estonia," *Rosbalt*, March 7, 2002.

49. "The Resource Wealth Burden—Oil and Gas Sectors in the Former USSR" (Warsaw: Center for Eastern Studies, December 2003), p. 60. http://www.osw.waw.pl/en/epub/eprace/12/aPRACE_12_do68_ang%20-%2027.01.pdf.

50. "Ukraine to Lose Economic Independence: Russian Oil Oligarchs Are Gaining Control over the Ukrainian Oil Industry," *Pravda*, June 24, 2003.

the agreement, both Transneft and Gazprom will set most of the terms and conditions, including volume, scheduling, and fees, for the transit of oil and gas to and through Ukraine. The deal was packaged to convince the Ukrainian public just before the October election that cheaper gasoline and fuel oil prices from Russia would be the result, but new minerals extraction and export taxes that go into effect in Russia on January 1, 2005, will negate any temporary price benefit accruing to the Ukrainian consumer. The agreement will also make more unlikely the construction of a pipeline through Ukraine that bypasses Russian territory.

None of the five countries has yet been able to develop import alternatives to Russian energy sources. In part this stems from the willingness of the Kremlin and Russian companies to undercut delivered prices of oil and gas that could be offered by any potential Western energy competitor. For example, Poland, which by law requires the government to pursue policies designed to develop alternative sources of energy imports, signed agreements in 2001 with Denmark and Norway to bring in natural gas via a proposed Baltic pipeline. At the time, the Poles were willing to pay a slight premium for Danish and Norwegian natural gas in order to have energy alternatives. Since those agreements, Gazprom dropped its price just enough to make the Baltic pipeline scheme unattractive. Norwegian gas prices also tend to follow changes in OPEC oil pricing more than does Russian gas, which gives the Russian companies a competitive edge. In addition, Danish and Norwegian companies are unwilling to price natural gas aggressively to allow them entry into new markets or to provide price breaks that serve foreign policy agendas. Needless to say, shareholders of Gazprom are not as demanding. Western companies may also be reluctant politically to move into areas that Gazprom considers to be its natural markets.

The countries of East Central Europe will gradually lose most of the financial benefit derived from buying Russian oil and gas. For political reasons, Ukraine will retain more advantages from its energy links with Russia, but at a steep political cost. In the past, the five countries considered here have paid approximately two-thirds of the price that Western consumers pay for a barrel of oil. With natural gas, the price difference has been almost 50 percent. The motivation of Russia's companies was in part a desire to lock in the markets of countries easily reached by Russia's pipeline systems. Nevertheless, even the short-term economic benefits to consumers in the Near Abroad should be weighed against their long-term interests in avoiding prolonged dependence on one country for their energy imports, particularly a country that traditionally has used its economic clout to dictate regional security policy.

The five countries have acquired some advantage and less dependence as they charge transit fees for Russian energy moving to third countries. Moscow, however, appears to have decided that Russia is more secure by not allowing itself to become dependent on other countries for pipeline routes. Under Putin, Russia is again pursuing autarkic economic policies, similar to those of the Soviet Union. During the mid-1980s, Russia was trying to become a major player in world energy markets at

---

51. "Russia and Ukraine Sign 15-Year Agreement on Oil Transit across the Territory of Ukraine," Interfax News Agency, August 18, 2004.

the same time that it was limiting imports to a few strategic items. Economic inter-dependence is favored by the reformers in the Kremlin but is resisted by the *siloviki* who are at the moment ascendant.

Russian Control of Energy Infrastructure

Large energy payment arrearages developed—particularly in Ukraine and Poland—during a short period following the breakup of the Soviet Union. In fairness to Gazprom, it should be noted that in the mid-1990s about 2.5 billion cubic meters of gas disappeared from Gazprom's pipes while crossing Ukraine.[52] These growing debts and thefts from pipelines were used by Russia to demand from Ukraine immediate payment of the arrearages; Ukraine's alternative was to grant compensation to Russia in the form of ownership of the country's energy facilities.

The Polish economy rebounded quickly enough to allow for the payment of all arrearages. In the Baltic states, it was Gazprom's custom to acquire a minority (but blocking) stake in a facility; this was followed by an incremental buyout of individual owners until majority ownership was acquired. Russian energy companies have now discovered that a gradual takeover is usually more politically acceptable within the importing country.

Gazprom is the undisputed champion when it comes to acquiring ownership of facilities in East Central Europe (see table 4 on page 32). The company currently owns between 34 and 40 percent of formerly state-owned gas companies in Estonia, Latvia, and Lithuania.[53] In Poland, 35 percent of Gas Trading is controlled by Gazprom, as is 48 percent of EuRoPol Gaz, which owns and controls the Yamal-Europe pipeline inside Poland.[54] In Ukraine, Gazprom has a minority share in the pipeline system, owns 51 percent of the large, gas equipment–manufacturing company Druzhkovskiy zavod gazovoi apparatury,[55] and is one of the largest foreign investors in Ukraine. Because of a lack of transparency in Gazprom's public documents, it is difficult to know exactly how much it has invested in non-gas-related projects in the five countries. Putin even selected Gazprom to take over Rosneft, thereby creating one of the largest energy conglomerates in the world.

LUKOIL is the second most important Russian company in the five countries (see table 5 on page 33). LUKOIL Baltija, which is 100 percent owned by LUKOIL, is the largest distributor of oil products in the three Baltic states. In Estonia, LUKOIL exports oil products via the ports of Tallinn and Muuga and has about 35 service stations in the country. In Latvia, LUKOIL has control of Latvijas Nafta, an independent retailer. It also operates a large petrochemical terminal at Ventspils. In addition, LUKOIL owns two small oil deposits in Latvia. LUKOIL has the largest number of service stations in Lithuania, with more than 100 retail outlets. LUKOIL attempted to take control of the large refinery at Mazeikiai, the port terminal at

52. Tatiana Koshkaaryova, "Each Day Ukraine Steals $5 Million from Russia," *Nezavisimaia Gazeta*, January 12, 1999.

53. "The Resource Wealth Burden," p. 60.

54. Ibid.

55. Ibid.

Table 4.   Gazprom[1] Activities in Selected Countries of the Near Abroad

Country & firm	Ownership of firm[2]	Main activity of firm
Estonia		
Eesti Gaas	37% Gazprom, 33% Ruhrgas, 10% Itera Latvija, 18% Fortum	Gas trading & transport
Latvia		
Latvijas Gaze	36% Ruhrgas, 25% Gazprom, 25% Itera, 12% E.ON Energie	Gas trading & transport (9% stock transfer expected from Itera Latvija To Gazprom)
Lithuania		
Stella Vitae	30% Gazprom	Gas trading
Lietuvos Dujos	35.7% Ruhrgas, 34% Gazprom, 24.36% state	State gas monopoly for gas distribution
Kaunas electric power plant	51% Gazprom	Electric power production
Poland		
EuRoPol GAZ	48% Gazprom, 48% PGNiG, 4% Polish Company	Gas trading; gas transport; owns Yamal-Europe pipeline inside Poland
Gas Trading	35% Gazprom	Gas trading
Ukraine		
Druzhkovskiy zavod gazovoi apparatury	51% Gazprom	Gas equipment manufacturing
Institut Yuzhniigiprogaz	40% Gazprom	Research Institute

1   Control of Gazprom: 38% state, 35% management, 15% private, 12% foreign.
2   Not all are totals.

Butinge, and the pipeline system, but lost out to YUKOS. As of mid-2004, however, it appears that YUKOS will be largely dismantled by the Russian government and either LUKOIL or a merged Gazprom/Rosneft group will be the leading contender to take over Lithuania's oil facilities.

YUKOS became a major player in the Baltic states in 2002 when it acquired majority control of Lithuania's oil facilities, including the Mazeikiai refinery, the port terminal, the pumping stations, and the pipeline from Belarus to the coast of the Baltic Sea (see table 6 on page 34). YUKOS became owner in an unusually transparent negotiation with the government of Lithuania and the Williams Companies, Inc., of Tulsa, Oklahoma, the previous general manager of the facilities. The Putin government's determination to dismantle YUKOS is a serious setback to creating greater trust in Russian business practices.

Table 5.   LUKOIL[1] Activities in Selected Countries of the Near Abroad

Country & firm	Ownership of firm[2]	Main activity of firm
Estonia		
LUKOIL Eesti	100% LUKOIL	Petrol stations, retail operations
Latvia		
LUKOIL Baltija	100% LUKOIL	Petrol stations, oil product transport
Lithuania		
LUKOIL Baltija	100% LUKOIL	32 petrol stations, wholesale and retail sales
LUKOIL D-6 Kravtsovskoe field	100% LUKOIL	Platform drilling of an estimated 600–700 million ton oil field in the Baltic Sea
Poland		
LUKOIL Polska Sp Z.O.O.	100% LUKOIL	130 gas stations
Ukraine		
LUKOIL Ukraine	100% LUKOIL	185 petrol stations
LUKOIL Odesa petroleum refinery	100% LUKOIL	Oil refinery at Odessa
Lukor	50% LUKOIL	Chemical and petrochemical production
Oriana	50% LUKOIL, 50% state	Petrochemical plant

Note: Getty Petroleum Marketing, in which LUKOIL has a 72 percent ownership stake, owns 1,200 gasoline stations in 12 U.S. states.

1   Control of LUKOIL: 89% management, 8% state, 3% private, 0.2% foreign.

2   Not all are totals.

In Poland, because of suspicion of Russian companies, LUKOIL has not yet been able to gain a significant foothold. Although LUKOIL has floated several proposals to buy the Gdansk refinery and the G-8 energy distributors in Poland, it has not yet been able to nail down the deal. YUKOS has been LUKOIL's major competitor for Gdansk, but its prospects have been greatly weakened by the actions of the Putin government. Some observers of the energy situation in Poland believe that LUKOIL's chances of a takeover have increased sharply, particularly if the facility is first privatized to one of the Polish oligarchs with close ties to Russian energy interests. The new Polish government is wary of putting Gdansk and other strategic energy facilities up for international tender, however, in part because it is aware that LUKOIL may be the only large bidder. For technical reasons, Polish oil refineries must receive at least 85 percent of their oil from Russia in order to operate at peak

Table 6.   YUKOS[1] Activities in Lithuania

Country & firm	Ownership of firm[2]	Main activity of firm
Lithuania		
Mazeikiai Nafta	53.7% YUKOS, 40.7% Lithuanian government	Oil refining/transportation complex, including Butinge terminal and Naftotiekis pipeline

1   Control of YUKOS: 61% Group Menatep, 24% publicly owned (domestic and foreign), 15% private.
2   Not a total.

capacity. Polish refineries are attempting to reduce this dependence on Russian crude, but the process is expensive and will take several years.

Kellogg, a U.S. engineering company, will be updating the Gdansk refinery to EU standards; in the process it will give the refinery the flexibility to meet EU standards by processing both sweeter crude or the heavy sulfur oil from the Urals. The upgrade may reduce somewhat Poland's dependence on the major Russian oil companies and allow it to deal with some smaller independents. The U.S. oil company, ConocoPhillips, may be interested in investing in Poland, but Poles are suspicious that Conoco's close relations with LUKOIL may result in a backdoor introduction of LUKOIL acquisition of local facilities. Before Conoco invests in Poland, it will have to be transparent about plans to partner with a Russian company. One well-informed Pole dismissed any Conoco interest in Poland, claiming that the company's representatives "only fly over Poland on their way to Russia." He contended that Russia was too important to U.S. companies for them to help Poland reduce its energy dependence on Russia.

LUKOIL, however, is now attempting to secure ownership in Grupa Lotos, which controls 25.6 percent of the Gdansk oil terminal, 12 percent of the Polish liquefied petroleum gas (LPG) market, and 130 gasoline stations. A Finnish study, done in 2003 by the Turku School of Economics, found that Poland, among new EU members, is the most attractive destination for Russian foreign direct investment (FDI). Almost all FDI in Poland so far is represented by equity investments made by Gazprom in manufacturing and distribution in the natural gas sector. A large part of Gazprom's investment comes from opaque bank accounts held in Cyprus.

The Poles, however, are more skeptical of Russian investment than are elites in Ukraine and Lithuania. Furthermore, Russia's cutoff of pipeline oil to Latvia in 2002 and gas to Belarus (some of which goes on to Poland) in 2004 has increased Warsaw's reluctance to allow Russian companies to buy out the large energy assets still held by the state. Janusz Steinhoff, a former minister of economics in Poland, said in an interview with the *Polish News Bulletin,* "Russian capital should be treated like any other; I wouldn't cast it as a villain. At the same time, Poland should guard itself against the domination of a single company (YUKOS).... The Russians are masters of long-term planning and are trying to win control over whole markets...."[56] Steinhoff was most likely referring indirectly to LUKOIL and Gazprom.

The Poles have almost completed planning for a small pipeline from Bernau to Szczecin that will be able to bring in 6 billion cubic meters of gas from Germany. The new Polish government of Prime Minister Marek Belka, which appears to be determined to look for ways to decrease Polish dependence on Russian supplies, is promoting construction of an alternative pipeline that would allow Poland to bring in supplies during any short-term cutoff of shipments from Russia. Much more work needs to be done by the Poles if an alternative pipeline is to become a reality.

Of course, the Poles are well aware that, in the aftermath of the current prosecution of the YUKOS leader, YUKOS will likely end up a more loyal instrument of Putin and Russia's power ministries. In addition, oil supplies for Poland's largest refineries, and particularly PKN Orlen's Plock facility, come from an offshore company registered in Cyprus and allegedly owned by two Ukraine-born musicians. The Poles recognize that their relative economic weakness and vulnerability to insider transactions are reasons they need to exercise greater caution when they deal with Russian companies than when they consider bids from legitimate Western firms. A Polish official confided that the government remains very concerned about pursuing privatization because it has no way at present of determining who is really behind many groups of investors, even if they are allegedly based in Western Europe.

Russian Ties with Former *Nomenklatura*

Poland

The collapse of the Soviet Union and the Warsaw Pact did not sever many of the personal ties that former Communist Party and industrial leaders had formed over the years. During the Cold War, all of the leaders in Eastern Europe learned to speak fluent Russian, and many of them owed their privileged positions to the sponsorship of Soviet leaders. Predictably, some individuals now in top political jobs are often the greatest opponents of business transparency. Poland's two wealthiest men developed their business skills during the Soviet period; after 1991, they established companies that became successful, in part, as a result of their close personal ties to Russian companies. Both men have also been substantial contributors to the ruling Social Democratic and Labor Party, which consists in large part of former members of the country's Soviet-era Communist Party.

One wealthy Polish energy executive started a company that became the monopoly importer of natural gas from Russia as a result of the owner's strong personal relations with the directors of Gazprom. At about the same time, Poland negotiated a take-or-pay agreement between the Polish government and Gazprom, which obligated Poland to accept larger quantities of natural gas than were needed. The deal was so one-sided that the Polish government has spent considerable effort trying to convince Gazprom to decrease the volume of gas exported to Poland.

---

56. "Government Report Warns of Russian Factor as Preparations for Orlen/MOL Merger Gather Pace," *Polish News Bulletin*, April 20, 2004.

The private Polish gas firm originally won the contract to construct the Yamal II pipeline. Because of Putin's support for the Baltic undersea gas pipeline, however, it is unlikely that Yamal II will be built anytime soon. Some in Poland believe that government has unnecessarily irritated Gazprom and the Russian Ministry of Industry and Energy by refusing to grant Gazprom the same kind of tax breaks that other foreign investors have received. Because of the opaque decisionmaking process in Moscow, it is difficult to judge whether the tax issue is an important factor in the case of Yamal II.

Discussing the possibility of securing alternative gas supplies through Ukraine, a private gas trader stated candidly, "Ukrainian companies depend on approval from Moscow. When one negotiates with a Ukrainian company, one has to realize that the real partner is in Moscow." The official also complained that Russians have not reformed their business practices as much as it is believed in Western Europe. This may or may not be an overly cynical view of the situation, but it does come from a person with long-established ties with Russian companies.

Meanwhile, another wealthy Polish industrial figure hoped to become even richer owing to his special relationship with Russian energy companies. He had almost succeeded in acquiring the Gdansk refinery through a winning bid submitted jointly with LUKOIL, but LUKOIL later backed off, citing the Polish entrepreneur's considerable transaction fee and demand for part control of the refinery. However, the entrepreneur has since been involved in various schemes with YUKOS and Hungary's MOL in a separate attempt to acquire the Gdansk refinery and other oil refinery and distribution assets that have been considered for privatization. Publicity regarding this entrepreneur's close ties with YUKOS gave the Polish government an additional incentive to put off privatizing more of the country's energy assets. The entrepreneur, however, continues to press for the sale of PKN to Petroval, a company believed to have close ties with YUKOS representatives in Western Europe.

Ukraine

In Ukraine, the same *nomenklatura* that ruled during Soviet days has predominant influence over the country's industrial policy. The three wealthiest and most politically influential people—President Kuchma; his son-in-law, Viktor Pinchuk; and the head of Naftohaz Ukrayiny, Yuri Boyko—are all connected to the energy industry. President Kuchma has particularly strong ties to LUKOIL; in fact he helped LUKOIL gain control of the Odessa refinery.

In addition, Kuchma has supported TNK-BP (see table 7 on page 37), Transneft, and the Russian government in their determination to block the construction of an east-west pipeline that would bypass Russia by carrying crude oil directly to Europe from the Caspian Sea via a pipeline from Odessa to Brody, and on to Plock in Poland. Viktor Pinchuk has financial interests in several refineries and chemical plants that depend on Russian crude oil supplies. Yuri Boyko reportedly owes his position and wealth to his close ties to Gazprom and the smaller spin-off, Itera. A Polish energy financier who prefers to remain anonymous has claimed that Boyko's ties to Gazprom and LUKOIL make him the key Ukrainian in terms of either building or blocking the construction of pipelines to the West.

Table 7. TNK-BP[1] Activities in Ukraine

Country & firm	Ownership of firm[2]	Main activity of firm
Ukraine		
TNK-Ukraine	100% TNK-BP	40 owned and 1006 franchised petrol stations
Linos refinery at Lisichansk	78% TNK-BP	Oil refinery

1 Control of TNK-BP: 50% Alfa Group/Acess-Renova Group [AAR], 50% BP.

2 Percentages are not totals.

The former Ukrainian prime minister, Pavlo Lazarenko, is being prosecuted in the United States on charges that he accepted $25 million from Itera in order to facilitate Itera's access to the Ukrainian market. Corruption in Ukraine's energy sector may be just as extensive as in Russia's, if not more so. The outgoing minister of industry and energy, Serhiy Yermilov, stated in an interview in early 2004 that Ukrtransnafta, the state oil company, actually represents the interests of Russia's Transneft by acting as middleman for the owners of Russian oil on Ukrainian territory and, in effect, serving criminal and Russian interests.[57] Several Ukrainian top officials, including a deputy prime minister, an energy minister, and the director of Ukrtransnafta, were dismissed during the first half of 2004 for opposing Russia's policies on the use of Ukrainian oil and gas pipelines.

The strange establishment in late 2002 of a small company in a village outside of Budapest, Hungary, illustrates the continued corruption of Russian energy companies in their quest to avoid transparency. Eural Trans Gas (ETG) was founded by a small group that the *Moscow Times* said comprised representatives of organized crime.[58] The new company's mission was to act as an intermediary between Gazprom and the two governments of Turkmenistan and Ukraine. Gazprom and its in-house bank, Gazprombank, granted ETG loans and guarantees of about $300 million simply to move Turkmen gas to Ukraine, an operation that Gazprom was easily suited to do by itself. In fact, ETG is simply another example of Gazprom's establishment of fictional competitors, the first being Itera. A venture the size of the ETG deal would not have been allowed to go forward without the approval of the PA, if not President Putin himself.

The creation of Itera and its registration in Jacksonville, Florida, allowed Gazprom to siphon off earnings to company managers and sympathetic Russian officials. Since 2002, Itera has lost much of its support in the Kremlin, and Gazprom has cut deeply into Itera's markets while it has established Itera-type daughter entities abroad. As we will see, however, any fictional notion of independent companies has now been dropped from Russian-Ukrainian energy relations.

57. "Ukraine's Ex-Minister of Fuel and Energy Goes Down with All Guns Blazing," BBC Monitoring Service, March 7, 2004.

58. Catherine Belton, "The Mob, an Actress, and a Pile of Cash," *Moscow Times*, November 27, 2004.

Latvia

Even in some of the Baltic states, the connection between wealth and energy is firmly established. In Latvia, the port of Ventspils is largely owned and controlled by the city's mayor, an ex-Communist. After the collapse of the Soviet Union, he was able to secure control of Ventspils, which until recently was the largest crude oil port in the Baltic states. Until the summer of 2002, when Transneft and LUKOIL cut the oil flow to Ventspils, the facility was a profit maker for the mayor and his business associates, many of whom had close ties to LUKOIL. Several influential politicians have financial connections to smaller Russian companies that transport oil to the Latvian coast via rail. Although Russian investment in Latvia is almost as large as Russian investment in Lithuania, ownership transparency is a larger problem in Latvia, making it more difficult to detect the extent of Russian control over the country's energy sector. Itera Latvia is headed by Juris Savickis, a well-known former KGB officer with no previous experience in the energy sector.

Although Russian investment in Latvia is almost as large as its investment in Lithuania (see the next section), ownership transparency is a larger problem in Latvia, making it more difficult to detect the extent of Russian control over the country's energy sector.

Lithuania

In Lithuania, Dujotekana, a Lithuanian-registered natural gas company located in Kleipeda, receives all its gas from Gazprom, which refers many potential customers to Dujotekana even though the smaller firm charges a premium for gas supplies. Gazprom has reserved 30 percent of the Lithuanian gas market for Dujotekana, a company owned by a few wealthy Lithuanians with strong ties to Russia. At one time or another, Gazprom has helped smaller Lithuanian gas distributors, such as Vikonda, Stella Vitae, Itera, and Dujotekana. Dujotekana is yet another example of how Gazprom facilitates the establishment of allegedly independent companies in order to funnel financial support to local political interests.

Lithuania may be as close to a Russian-dominated energy economy as exists anywhere outside of Ukraine. Some of the country's top political figures have had extremely close ties with LUKOIL CEO Vagit Alekperov and other executives of that company. By 1998, the directors of the Mazeikiu Refinery, the Birzai pipeline terminal, and the new Butinge port facility were all individuals close to LUKOIL. In that year, there were more LUKOIL than Lithuanian flags flying around the Mazeikiu Refinery, even though LUKOIL had no financial stake in the facility. Gazprom had also established close ties with many of the same political figures. A few months before the 2000 parliamentary elections, the leading candidate for prime minister unsuccessfully attempted to keep secret a private trip to Moscow to consult with Gazprom regarding the company's desire to buy into Lithuania's gas monopoly.

One of Lithuania's wealthiest industrial leaders owns the country's major port and largest chemical plant. He started his career during the independence period with the support of Russia's oil and gas traders. He has been one of the country's largest individual contributors to Lithuania's political parties, from the Social Democrats (former Communists) on the left to the conservative Home Land Party on the right. Another of the country's wealthiest individuals and now a member of the government was active in Lithuania (after emigrating from Russia in 1985) in brokering Russian gas shipments through Itera and later had a stake in Dujotekana. In 1999, this businessman/politician represented TNK in its attempt to win the right to buy the country's oil infrastructure. Thus, Russia's energy wealth and political power are deeply embedded in Lithuania, the Baltic state with the smallest ethnic Russian population.

Money, Energy, and Politics

It is difficult for an outsider to chart the flow of energy money into politics, particularly in countries that lack enforcement of tough campaign finance laws. Close connections among Russian energy companies, intelligence services of former Communist countries, and current political figures also impede information gathering. In addition, Russian embassies in former Communist countries are sometimes channels for funneling energy money into politics. Almost every member of the political and business elite in the five countries studied here can recite specific instances of individuals taking bribes or illegal campaign financing from Russian companies. These local politicians and businesspeople usually (but not always) come up short, however, when asked for hard evidence of illegal money flows. Although money laundering still exists in developed Western states, the use of cooperating banks and institutions in Central European countries is more commonly used for the transfer abroad of large sums of money earned from Russian energy exports.

The corrupting influence of Russian companies on the democratic processes in the five countries is strongly indicated, however. In April 2003 Latvia's Corruption Combating and Prevention Bureau suspended the leader of the country's National Harmony Party for failure to notify the bureau of several financial contributions, some of which are believed to have come from Russian sources.[59] In Lithuania, the parliamentary campaign of 2000 was openly influenced by money contributed by Vaizga, a shell company set up by Ivan Palechek, manager of LUKOIL Baltija. Known contributions are only the tip of the LUKOIL iceberg as it rewards friendly politicians. Latvian government sources are convinced that Vaizga contributed funds to some of Latvia's left-wing political groups. In less-transparent Ukraine, however, Russian companies make little effort to hide their ties to cooperating political leaders.

According to the Lithuanian Parliamentary Special Commission, Rolandas Paksas, the recently impeached president and twice-resigned prime minister of Lithuania, was heavily financed by Yuri Borisov, a Russian citizen residing in Lithuania who reputedly has ties to Russian military intelligence. The same commission was also reportedly given recordings of phone conversations that prove that Paksas was assisting LUKOIL in taking over energy facilities in Lithuania.[60] Paksas

---

59. Madara Licite, "TSP Submitted Incomplete Financial Declaration due to Lack of Information," Latvian News Agency, April 24, 2003.

was also forced to admit that he had received political contributions from Almax, a Kaliningrad company that the commission believes has ties to Russian intelligence.

During negotiations in 1999 among the government of Lithuania, the Williams Companies, and LUKOIL, Paksas, who was then the prime minister, appointed Eugenijus Maldeikis as minister of economy. Maldeikis had particularly close relations with LUKOIL, and soon after he resigned his ministerial appointment after a change of government, he visited LUKOIL headquarters several times. At the time, Paksas admitted that the resignation of his government was an attempt to stop a Lithuanian agreement with Williams. The obvious beneficiary of the failure of making a deal with Williams in 1999 was LUKOIL.

60. Nick Patton Walsh, "Lithuania Axes President in Phone Tap Row: MPs Dismiss Eccentric Leader over Ties with Russian Backer," *Guardian*, April 7, 2004, p. 12.

CHAPTER 6

Russia Plays Its Energy Card

Russia has been a clever player of the energy game in neighboring countries and on specific issues such as the Odessa-Brody pipeline and electricity supply.

Lithuania: LUKOIL and Williams

From 1998 to 2000, Lithuania exemplified the linkage of Russian energy and politics. During the prolonged negotiations among the Williams Companies, the Lithuanian government, and LUKOIL, LUKOIL on nine different occasions was able to persuade Transneft and the Russian Ministry of Industry and Energy to cut off the flow of oil to Lithuania through the large pipeline that runs through Belarus to the Lithuanian port terminal at Butinge, with a large spur running northwest to the Latvian port of Ventspils. At the time of each cutoff, LUKOIL's supporters in Lithuania pointed to the stoppage as proof that Williams was not an effective partner for LUKOIL. It was a surprise that in Lithuania—unlike Ukraine—few politicians criticized Russia for shutting off the oil, a possible indication of Russian influence with Lithuanian elites.

The government at that time (Conservative and Christian Democrats), believing that a large investment by a U.S. energy company would enhance security and help Lithuania gain accession to NATO, supported the deal with Williams. The opposition (Democratic Labor Party and Social Democratic Party) argued that an agreement with Williams would ignore the natural interests of Russian companies and their ability to participate in the Lithuanian oil market. The opposition also claimed that the Williams Company was strong-arming Lithuania into selling its energy assets at below value and that a deal would severely damage Lithuania's economy and the country's ability to control its sovereignty. Williams recognized from the start that it could not operate in Lithuania without a long-term crude oil supply agreement with one of the Russian majors. The U.S. company also saw that this would be impossible without granting a Russian company a share of the equity ownership.

Before 1997, LUKOIL had managed to secure effective control over all the facilities without making a significant investment in plant modernization. When it became apparent in 1999 that LUKOIL might not gain legal ownership or management control of the facilities, Moscow—with the support of LUKOIL—replaced the Russian ambassador to Lithuania with an intelligence officer whom they hoped would be of more help in securing control of Lithuania's oil infrastructure. The new ambassador was Yuri Zubakov, a 25-year veteran of the KGB who had spent the previous year as liaison officer between the KGB and LUKOIL.

Zubakov, who had never before been assigned outside Russia, confirmed his KGB background in private conversations with his new diplomatic colleagues in Vilnius and never issued a statement denying his intelligence background when it was exposed in the Lithuanian press.

Not long after Zubakov's arrival, the Williams Company and its supporters in Lithuania discovered that the number of negative press articles and rumors spread by opposing parliamentarians increased significantly. It became clear that Zubakov had been assigned the task of stopping Williams from replacing LUKOIL as the dominant partner for Lithuania's oil industry. Nevertheless, the Lithuanian negotiations did not follow the script that LUKOIL had written: YUKOS in 1999 was able to secure Kremlin (and Lithuanian) approval to conclude a deal with Williams. The agreement was acceptable to the Conservative government of Andres Kubilius because the Conservative Party was one of the few that lacked close ties to LUKOIL.[61]

After Zubakov's 1999 arrival in Vilnius, Ivan Palechek, manager of LUKOIL's local distributor, LUKOIL Baltija, established an allegedly independent company called Vaizga that funneled campaign finance money to various political groups.

During the 2000 election in Lithuania, Vaizga was the largest financial supporter of political parties that opposed the government's negotiations with Williams. Vaizga contributed at least 360,000 litas ($90,000) to the political campaign: 150,000 litas to the Social Democratic Party; 35,000 litas to another opponent, the New Democratic Party; and 25,000 litas to the Russian Union.[62] Again, the number of negative articles in the Lithuanian press increased notably, as did statements by several political figures regarding the alleged nefarious intentions of Williams and charges that the investment of the U.S. firm would severely damage Lithuania's economy and the country's ability to control its own sovereignty.

LUKOIL certainly expected to benefit in the negotiations by having a sympathetic former KGB officer as Russia's ambassador to Lithuania in the crucial year 1999. LUKOIL and its supporters in Lithuania overplayed their hand, however, and Williams and the Conservatives were able to open negotiations with YUKOS. For its part, Williams was able to quickly finish construction of the Butinge terminal, thereby enabling the Americans to temporarily import crude from the world spot market. Even though imports through Butinge depended on purchases from non-Russian sources and were more costly than piped oil from Russia, this reverse flow gave Lithuania an ability to keep the refinery working, thereby undercutting the effect of LUKOIL's disruptions in supply and time to negotiate an acceptable agree-

---

61. Following his three-year assignment to Lithuania, Zubakov was assigned to Moldova, which had an energy industry almost entirely controlled by LUKOIL and Gazprom. LUKOIL's use of a KGB officer to openly promote its interests abroad was unusual. Although Russian energy companies such as Zarubezhneft, Transneft, Gazprom, and Rosneft have hired many former intelligence officers, it is rare that Moscow sends out a known KGB veteran to a diplomatic post in order to directly influence a commercial negotiation. Zubakov's assignment highlights the importance the Kremlin attaches to maintaining control over key energy facilities in Russia's neighborhood.

62. "Oil Companies Supported Lithuania's Left Wing Opposition in Elections," Baltic News Service, November 9, 2000.

ment with YUKOS, which had by that time developed its own political backers in Moscow.

A major question is what will happen to Lithuania's port of Butinge once pressure is exerted on the exporters to fill the Primorsk pipeline. Lithuanians are rightly concerned, but because a Russian company owns the infrastructure and thus provides the Kremlin with some political leverage, the port will likely be preserved as an export route for crude from the southern Urals. The deal with YUKOS was clearly more an advantage for Lithuania than turning over the facilities to LUKOIL would have been.

Although in 1974 the Soviet Union ratified the Helsinki Convention regarding drilling or production activity that might affect the Baltic Sea area, LUKOIL—in violation of the convention—has ignored the convention's requirements in its plans to drill for oil only 22 kilometers off Lithuania's Curonian Spit and 7 kilometers from the Lithuanian-Russian maritime border.[63] The Curonian Spit, which has a land border with Kaliningrad, is on UNESCO's World Heritage List and is part of an extremely fragile ecosystem. Since 2000, the Lithuanian government has asked Russia to hold up operations until an international group can examine the environmental impact. LUKOIL has refused to do so and has proceeded with exploratory drilling for the $270 million project. LUKOIL plans to start production from the field in late 2004, extract 70,000 tons by the end of 2004, and attain an output of 600,000 tons a year by 2007.[64]

In March of 2004, the leaders of Denmark, Sweden, Finland, and the three Baltic countries called on Russia to stop the drilling off the coast of Lithuania. The Putin government could easily require LUKOIL to comply with the Lithuanian request. Nevertheless LUKOIL is, in part, using the incident to pressure Lithuania into allowing LUKOIL to build an oil pipeline across Lithuania to Kaliningrad that will be entirely under Russian control—a situation that would be anathema to any Western country.

Latvia: The Saga of Ventspils

The port of Ventspils, in Latvia, is the largest oil terminal on the Baltic Sea and, until recently, Russia's second-largest export port for Russian oil.[65] The Latvian port can handle 16 million tons a year of crude. In addition, the port can be readily expanded to export larger volumes of Russian crude or refined product. In 2002, however, the owners of the port of Ventspils rejected a purchase offer from Transneft and LUKOIL to buy them out, and offer transmitted more as a nonnegotiable demand than as a friendly takeover. Almost immediately, Transneft let it be known that no Russian crude would be carried by pipeline to Ventspils until a sale was negotiated that would give a working majority of the shares to a Russian company.

63. "Helsinki Convention on the Protection of the Marine Environment of the Baltic Sea, 1992," www.helcom.fi/helcom/convention.html.

64. Press release by Kaliningradmorneft (a LUKOIL subsidiary), July 20, 2004, www.LUKOIL-kmn.com/release.phtml?id=35&PHPSESSID=9ae3f7dfd33b95e3f84ea8c0c9ae3d3c.

65. The Caspian harbor of Novorossiisk is the largest.

Until the cutoff, Latvians were collecting about $200 million a year in transit fees. Although substantial amounts of Russian crude are still delivered by rail to Ventspils, the crude comes mainly from "stranded fields" that are not yet connected to the present pipeline system. However, the smaller Russian companies that have been sending crude by rail to Ventspils are increasingly under pressure to finance interconnecting pipelines to the BPS. The squeeze on Latvia appears to be tightening. The costs of shipping crude oil by rail are considerably higher than by pipe, and transit fees have been reduced by Latvia in order to make this route economically more attractive. Nevertheless, in April of 2004, the Ventspils offloading of diesel fuel dropped by 50 percent from a year earlier.

The Russian government and its companies have taken a hard line with the Latvians. A Moscow-based executive of one Russian oil company stated confidently that Latvians will eventually bow to Transneft-LUKOIL demands regarding ownership.[66] On the other hand, a senior executive of YUKOS commented in Moscow: "Ventspils is dead, or will be within two years."[67] Simyon Weinshtok, president of Transneft, in September 2003 said, "Russia will no longer engage in charity with the Baltic countries on problems dealing with oil transportation."[68]

Weinshtok is well aware that construction of the Primorsk refinery increases his leverage over Latvia as well as the other two Baltic states. Even before the Primorsk construction and the weakening of YUKOS, Transneft was increasing its already tight control over the oil export trade. From 2002 to 2003, Transneft was able to cut by half the amount of exported oil that was transported independent of Transneft, including by rail and water.[69] Transneft and Gazprom have increasingly become Putin's energy companies of choice whenever he needs willing instruments of his foreign policy.

In July 2004, the Kremlin announced that it was sending Victor Kaluzhny to Riga as the new Russian ambassador to Latvia. Kaluzhny was Russia's minister of fuel and energy in 1999. He has also been a close friend of a senior official of LUKOIL for more than 25 years and has long supported LUKOIL's operations inside and outside of Russia. In 1999, Kaluzhny sent letters to all of Russia's oil companies asking that they cut off all oil shipments to Lithuania in support of LUKOIL's attempt to take over that country's oil infrastructure and prevent the sale of the facilities to Williams.[70] The Latvians have little doubt that Kaluzhny was appointed to push for the acquisition of the port of Ventspils by LUKOIL. Some in Riga speculate that the Russian government is concerned that it may not be able to construct pipelines fast enough to move the increased oil production to Western markets— and thereby take advantage of the present high world market prices—without the Baltic ports of Butinge and Ventspils. This may be wishful thinking.

---

66. Executive of Russian oil company, comment to author, June 2003.

67. Senior executive of YUKOS, comment to author, June 2003.

68. Gherman Solomatin and Dmitry Zlodorev, "Russia Not to Engage in Charity with Baltic Countries on Oil," ITAR-TASS World Service, September 23, 2003.

69. "Oil Shipment via Port of Primorsk up 20.8 percent on Year in Jan–Oct," Prime-TASS Energy Service, November 11, 2003.

70. Dmitrii Mironov, "Biography: Viktor Ivanovich Kaluzhny," *Profil´*, August 2, 1999, www.grankin.ru/archiv/profil020899-58.htm.

Weinshtok's statements reflect the Putin government's determination to use only Russian transit routes and Russian ports whenever possible, even when this results in significantly higher transport costs. This Russian position is particularly evident in the Baltics, where the policy is reinforced by President Putin's strong personal animus against the three former Soviet republics. Putin has not forgotten that his father was captured by Estonians during World War II and turned over to German troops. In addition, as a native of St. Petersburg (and an admirer of Peter the Great), Putin believes that the Baltic states have historically been, and should remain, an integral part of Russia. In addition, Mrs. Putin is from Russia's Baltic enclave of Kaliningrad and is active in trying to keep the Russian language alive in the three former republics of the Soviet Union. Therefore, the Baltic states wisely expect no favors from Putin and his advisers.

Putin has for several years been one of strongest backers in Russia of the project to build a major oil port at Primorsk, close to St. Petersburg. He supported this project even when he was deputy mayor of St. Petersburg. Although Primorsk opened for business only in late 2001, by 2003 it was already shipping out 360,000 barrels of day. Exports were targeted at 840,000 barrels of oil per day for March 2004, and Transneft anticipates increasing shipments to 1.1 million barrels per day by the end of 2004.[71]

Within two years Primorsk may be capable of handling 1.2 million barrels a day. This would allow Russia to bypass all of the Baltic states when it exports crude oil to Europe. Energy professionals in the Baltic states speculate that the Russian Ministry of Transportation will increase rail tariffs, with the goal of putting additional pressure on the smaller Russian oil companies to link up with the Primorsk pipeline system. One Polish energy expert charged, ". . .the Baltic Pipeline System demonstrates that the Russians are not averse to spending extra money to punish countries or just to screw them out of revenue." Russia can hardly be faulted for wanting to increase its export capacity to Western Europe and even the United States quickly; nevertheless, pipeline economics alone would warrant using existing Baltic ports to the greatest extent possible.

Over the next few years, however, it may become clear that it was not in Russia's best economic interests to shut off the almost always ice-free port of Ventspils from piped crude export. Crude oil prices may well remain in the $40–$45 per barrel range, making the loss of the Ventspils route costly to the Russian treasury. If the construction of a proposed export route to the Barents Sea—whether through Murmansk or Indiga—is delayed, increased production in the West Siberian fields may present capacity problems in the winter, even for a greatly expanded Primorsk. Attempting to starve Ventspils into selling cheap to Transneft may turn out to be more expensive for Russia than for Latvia.

As of late May 2004, Putin was openly complaining to Transneft chief, Simyon Weinshtok, about the lack of export pipeline space needed to capitalize on today's unprecedented high oil prices.[72] Transneft was running at full capacity but was still

71. "Russia Cuts Black Sea Loadings in February," Energy Intelligence Group, Inc., January 26, 2004.
72. Catherine Belton, "Putin: Move Faster on Pipelines," *Moscow Times*, May 27, 2004.

unwilling to pipe crude out through Ventspils, a policy ironically supported by Putin. This is another good example of politics trumping economics in Russia's energy patch. It is possible that Putin's complaints were made for the benefit of oil importers, including the United States, which have been pushing Moscow hard for export growth in the face of prices greater than $40 per barrel.

Some Russian economists—after accounting for the construction cost of pipelines and storage facilities, the longer shipping route to European markets, and delays from ice outside Primorsk during part of the winter—have questioned the costs of shipping through Primorsk. Not surprisingly, the port of Ventspils board chairman, Aivars Lembergs, continues to assert that shipping crude oil out through Ventspils would save Russian companies almost $8 a ton.[73]

Because winter ice hinders attracting foreign shippers, Russia is planning to spend considerable additional funds to build an undersea pipeline to the Finnish port of Porvoo and also barge oil to an offshore tanker outside the area of Primorsk that freezes in the winter.

Although the loss of transit revenue should not be a serious long-term financial problem for the three economically fast-growing Baltic states—GDP growth has averaged 5–7 percent annually during the past three years[74]—some Russians hope and believe that diverting exports to Primorsk will cause major pain in Latvia and Estonia. In the long run, however, it will decrease rather than increase Russian influence, in part by accelerating the shift of Latvian trade from east to west. The owners of Ventspils have already been able to shift some of the capacity of the port facility to the export of nonoil products such as wheat and coal. However, because the wheat and coal come from Russia, the Kremlin will retain its ability to cut many of its financial and commercial links with Latvia, as it did in mid-1998 after a political dispute with Latvia over ethnic Russian pensioners.

Another disadvantage of Primorsk over Ventspils (and Butinge) is the environmental impact of the longer shipping route from the Russian port. Sweden, Estonia, and Finland have already raised concerns about the prospect of 60 million tons of crude moving through the relatively crowded and inclement Gulf of Finland. Memories are still fresh in those countries of the sinking in September 1994 of the ferry *Estonia*, with the loss of more than 900 lives. The Danes are also concerned about the increasing tanker traffic through the Danish strait although this would be a concern even if the increased export of crude were to transit Baltic ports.

A new issue has surfaced, however, which could in the short run benefit Latvia and the port of Ventspils. In June 2004, Latvia objected to the EU's approval of Russia's WTO membership, citing Russia's "discriminatory railway tariffs and access to energy resources." Latvia's objection caught Moscow off guard when it charged in Geneva that Russian tariffs and Transneft's embargo of Ventspils are designed to choke off exports through the Latvian port. In late 2004, Moscow's reaction to the Latvian objection to Russia's WTO membership is not clear.

---

73. *Alexander's Gas & Oil Connections* 9, no. 7 (April 7, 2004).
74. World Bank Data & Statistics: Europe and Central Asia Online, web.worldbank.org.

Ukraine: *Siloviki* and Oligarchs

Shortly after Russia's failure in 1992 to maintain its military presence in the Baltic states, the Kremlin achieved more success in its efforts to extract political concessions from Ukraine. The Massandra incident, as it became known, started as an attempt by the Yeltsin government to force Kyiv to pay debts incurred as a result of previous gas exports from Russia. The Russian right to recover arrearages was legitimate, but it quickly became apparent that Moscow saw this as an opportunity to use its energy muscle to extract political concessions from the Ukrainian government. One week before a scheduled summit between President Yeltsin and President Kravchuk of Ukraine in early September 1993, Gazprom reduced its supplies of natural gas to Ukraine by 25 percent.[75] Most of Ukraine's public buildings turned off their heating, Kyiv turned off its streetlights, and television stations broadcast on reduced schedules.

Although Gazprom cited Ukrainian debt as the only reason for the cutoff, the Russian delegation at the summit meeting stated that the gas debt could be cancelled if Ukraine would cede full control over the Black Sea fleet to Russia and turn over its remaining nuclear warheads to the Russian Strategic Rocket Forces. Kravchuk was told that if his government did not accept the demands, all gas shipments would be blocked. Although Kravchuk initially agreed to Moscow's terms, the political fallout in Ukraine was great enough to force the president to backtrack to a settlement giving Gazprom 51 percent ownership in the gas pipeline transiting Ukraine, which opened the door to further Russian acquisition of gas and chemical facilities in Ukraine.

Nevertheless, only two years later, in 1995, Russia placed new excise duties on Ukraine's oil and gas imports, demanding that Ukraine pay prices higher than world market prices for its energy imports. Here again, Ukrainian gas debt was cited as the reason for this drastic move; and, here again, the solution was a political one in favor of Ukraine's more powerful neighbor: The duties would be lifted by Moscow if Ukraine agreed to join the Russia, Belarus, and Kazakhstan customs union. For a telling illustration of Russia's deals with Ukraine, one Russian journalist, Yuliya Mostovaya, in a 2000 article in *Zerkalo Nedeli*, quoted a "very competent source": "We [Russia] will sell you [Ukraine] five billion cubic meters of gas, and you enter the CIS customs union; we sell you an additional five billion cubic meters, and you support our position on the issue of the ABM treaty."

Citing Ukraine's outstanding debt as the reason, Russia from December 1999 to February 2000 again halted oil shipments to Ukraine. Even the Russian economic newspaper, *Vedomosti*, claimed that the blockade was motivated by the desire of Russian companies to gain leverage during the forthcoming privatization of the rest of Ukraine's pipeline system.[76] As a result of the negative publicity directed against Moscow over its tough tactics, the Kremlin has apparently decided that it could bet-

---

75. Paul J. D'Anieri, *Economic Interdependence in Ukrainian-Russian Relations* (Albany: State University of New York Press, 1999), 78.

76. Tor Bukkvoll, "Off the Cuff Politics: Explaining Russia's Lack of a Ukraine Strategy," *Europe-Asia Studies* 53, no. 8 (December 2001): 1144.

ter achieve the same political objectives in Ukraine by shifting its strategy. Instead of public threats, Moscow now uses more subtlety in its foreign energy policies—quiet corruption combined with pressure on elites to acquire greater ownership of Ukraine's strategic energy sector.

Poland: The Dangers of Privatization

Russian oil companies have had more difficulty projecting their energy influence over Poland. Repeated attempts by LUKOIL and YUKOS to buy the Gdansk refinery, the PKN Orlen energy complex, and the G-8 refineries have been stymied by Polish suspicion of increased dependence on Russia by private domestic interests who themselves want to gain control of the facilities and by political indecision stemming from divisions within Poland's governing coalitions. Nevertheless, Gazprom has been successful in dominating the gas transit market and in establishing close ties to some political leaders.

Most Poles can cite examples of Russia using its energy monopoly for economic and financial advantage in Poland, but few can provide evidence that Russian pressure has yet had a measurable impact on Polish foreign or security policies. Some Poles, who have been close to the country's intelligence community, are convinced that the governing Social Democrats receive indirect funding from Russian energy companies and that a few Polish companies have close ties with Russian firms and intelligence agencies.[77] It is no surprise that little hard evidence—in public sources, at least—exists to support this contention.

Energy specialists in Poland's private sector complain, however, that frequent shifts in government have brought in ministers who lack sufficient knowledge of the energy market and expertise in negotiating with Russian companies.[78] Russian negotiators usually have greater knowledge than Polish negotiators of international energy markets and pipeline issues and have internalized a tougher, zero-sum negotiating culture. For example, a former Russian minister of restructuring played a key role in negotiating an agreement between Gazprom and Poland that restricted incoming gas lines to three Gazprom-controlled border cities. This prevents smaller Russian companies from supplying Poland with more competitively priced gas. These restrictions also prevent Poland from importing gas from Turkmenistan, Kazakhstan, and other Caspian sources.

Because the Poles remain contractually obligated to take or pay for more natural gas from Russia than they need, some Polish officials hope that the European Commission will support their contention that, as EU members, they are in a single market. Therefore, they should be able to reexport and sell to other markets excess quantities of Russian gas. Of course, Moscow opposes this interpretation of what Poland can do as an EU member, and officials of the European Commission's Directorate General for Energy and Transport (DG TREN) are reluctant for political rather than legal reasons to back Warsaw on this issue.

---

77. Polish government official, interview with author, May 2004.
78. Polish energy consultant, interview with author, May 2004.

Poles also hope, perhaps unrealistically, that building a westward extension of the Odessa-Brody oil pipeline would allow the construction of a parallel gas pipeline that would ship oil in both directions. Underlying Warsaw's negotiations is the attainment of Western political support by tying into a system that also feeds into Western Europe. Poland would then have diversified access to non-Russian gas from the Caspian region.

Poles are also hoping that Ukrainians will elect a more Western-oriented government. If Kyiv then cooperates with Poland in efforts to secure gas from smaller Russian companies, these companies may be able to undercut Gazprom or Itera on price. Poland would like to receive gas in the amount of at least 5 billion cubic meters a year through Ukraine. This hope is unlikely to be fulfilled anytime soon, however, because of the continued strength of pro-Russian business clans in Ukraine and Putin's inflexibility over allowing strong Russian competitors to Gazprom.

With the help of so-called partners in the West who have nontransparent ownership structures, both LUKOIL and YUKOS have tried to buy the Gdansk refinery. Polish suspicions of Russian pipeline policies are certainly understandable. After construction of the giant Yamal I gas pipeline system, which transits Belarus and Poland to Germany, the Poles were surprised to discover that Gazprom had, without authorization, installed a fiber-optic cable system alongside the gas pipe. The cable was of such high capacity that it could handle all telecommunications traffic between Russia and Western Europe. Gazprom's agent, Europol Gaz, had assumed—rightly as it turned out—that it would be able to conceal the cable system until it was too late for the Polish government to either stop the cable installation or charge user or transit fees.

Gazprom has pressured Poland to accept the cable installation and focus instead on securing additional transit revenue through the construction of Yamal II, a parallel pipeline that would send additional gas to Germany. In anticipation of the construction of the second pipeline, Polish companies have already completed the engineering for additional pumping stations for Yamal I and for the proposed Yamal II. As of mid-2004, however, Gazprom, with the strong backing of President Putin, has decided instead to construct under the Baltic Sea a gas pipeline—sometimes referred to as the North European Pipeline—that would go directly from Russia to Germany, bypassing Poland. Constructing this pipeline would significantly delay, or possibly eliminate, the need for Yamal II. The cost of the undersea pipeline is conservatively estimated at three to four times the cost of Yamal II. Poles are convinced that the undersea project is Putin's way of demonstrating to Poland and Belarus that Russia is prepared to invest large sums of money to display Russia's energy dominance and eliminate the possibility that Poland or Belarus could use additional pipelines as leverage with Moscow.

Poles are disappointed that Chancellor Gerhard Schröder of Germany and President Jacques Chirac of France are supporting the undersea Baltic bypass, for the bypass would be built primarily for noneconomic reasons. Transit fees from Poland and Belarus over a 20-year period would cost less than the additional price of building the undersea system. Poles suspect that the Germans and French are going along with Putin in the expectation that their companies will be given preference in acquiring shares in Russia's domestic oil and gas industry. One former Polish official was told by a Russian intelligence officer that the undersea route will demonstrate that "Poland will not be rewarded for joining NATO." It is noteworthy that the Poles have always paid their oil and gas debts to Russia fully and in a timely fashion.

In April 2004, Poles and Lithuanians were shocked when their supplies of Russian natural gas were shut off as a result of a Gazprom feud with the Belarus government of Alexander Lukashenko. Gazprom has several times interrupted gas supplies to Belarus because of nonpayment or because of Minsk's unwillingness or inability to pay substantially higher fees for Russian gas supplies. When Gazprom's hardball tactics directly affected Poland and Lithuania, both countries asked Russia to compensate them for damages to their economies. Gazprom, supported by Russia's Ministry of Industry and Energy, rejected the requests, declaring that they were certain that no significant harm had been done to the two countries and, therefore, compensation payments were unnecessary.

Odessa-Brody Pipeline: Part of the Great Game

The Odessa-Brody pipeline project to Poland and Germany, known as the Eurasian Transportation Corridor (EATC), is only the latest example of Russian hardball tactics used to block oil flows and thereby dominate the energy policies of a neighbor. The project, which is particularly important to the Poles, would have taken Caspian crude oil from the Azerbaijan port of Baku, to the Black Sea port of Supsa in Georgia, and then to Ukraine's port of Odessa by tanker; from Odessa it would be piped to Brody (also in Ukraine) and continue through Poland to Western Europe. Moscow has been determined to stop the development of any oil or gas pipelines to the West that bypass Russian territory. Russian political leaders have been unhappy about their failure to prevent the construction of the Baku-Tiblisi-Ceyhan pipeline, a project that was pushed hard by the United States.

Source: U.S. Department of Energy, Energy Information Administration.

The Kremlin worked effectively to prevent the extension to Poland of the Odessa-Brody line, which would have carried Caspian oil, and to reverse the flow of oil—Russian oil in this case—from Brody to Odessa. Russia's ambassador to Ukraine, Viktor Chernomyrdin (formerly head of Gazprom as well as prime minister and energy czar under Yeltsin), on Ukrainian television once called Odessa-Brody "a bone in my throat."[79] He and Putin have made killing the project their personal priorities in Russia's relations with Ukraine. President Putin and President

---

79. Ukrainian government official, interview with author, April 2004.

Kuchma met at least nine times during the first eight months of 2004, and on each occasion Putin pushed hard for a stronger role for Russia's energy interests in Ukraine. In 2003, when Ukraine proposed increasing Russian transit of oil through the southern fork of the Druzhba pipeline that runs to the Adriatic Sea, Ukraine was surprised to be told that any agreement on volume increases was contingent on reversing the flow of the Odessa-Brody line to the benefit of TNK-BP.

Supporters of the Odessa-Brody line within Ukrtransnafta, the Ukrainian state pipeline firm, have expressed fears for their personal safety; and the major supporter of Odessa-Brody within the company, Oleksandr Todiychuk—the special plenipotentiary of Ukraine on the Euro-Asia Oil Transportation Corridor—was sacked by Kuchma in May 2004. This followed the firing by Kuchma of a deputy prime minister and a minister of fuel and energy during the previous year, reportedly over the ministers' support for construction of the pipeline bypassing Russia.

Although in the spring of 2004 Kuchma had assured the Poles of his support for a westward extension of Odessa-Brody, it is apparent he has been under intense pressure from Putin to change his position. In early July 2004, Kuchma officially reversed the decision of his government and declared that TNK would be allowed to fill the existing Odessa-Brody line and ship Russian crude to the port of Odessa. Although the agreement can be revised to re-reverse the flow from Odessa to Brody, U.S. and EU officials believe that the August agreement with Russia will delay any westward use of the pipeline for several years. By then,

Source: U.S. Department of Energy, Energy Information Administration.

TNK and the Russian Ministry of Industry and Energy hope that the project's supporters will become more dependent on Russian routes and will lose financial interest in the Ukrainian bypass of Russia.

Some Western observers and officials of Ukrtransnafta believe that Kuchma has been playing a game with Western governments and energy companies. They believe that he has, for political reasons, dangled before them the prospect of a westward extension of the pipeline but that he made a commitment to Putin in late 2003 to favor TNK-BP's use of the line to ship crude to the Black Sea.

Latvian officials and representatives of Ukrtransnafta report privately that the Kazakhstan government in early 2004 expressed interest in using the Odessa-Brody pipeline to ship oil in the amount of more than 150,000 barrels a day from the developing Kashagan field directly to European markets once exports start. KazMunaiGaz (KMG) pledged to carry out a feasibility study. ChevronTexaco, a major player in the Kazakh sector of the Caspian Sea, conducted extensive talks about the project with the Kazakhs, Ukrainians, and Poles. Latvians and Ukrainians reported that shortly after Kazakhstan expressed interest, Putin warned President Nursultan Nazarbayev that Russian-Kazakh relations would be damaged if Kazakhstan supported the bypass. The Azeris have also indicated their interest in sending crude through a westward extension of Odessa-Brody. The project is not financially attractive, however, without a guarantee of the large volumes of crude that the Kazakhs will be able to generate in 2007 or 2008.

The West interpreted the reversal as a sign that Kuchma yielded to pressure by Putin, whose support could be crucial to presidential aspirant Viktor Yanukovich in the October-November 2004 elections. Kuchma's decision was a great disappointment to the EU and the United States. The U.S. Department of Energy is convinced that reversing the flow to the benefit of TNK will effectively kill the pipeline as a means for Caspian oil to reach Western Europe. The U.S. embassy in Kyiv reports that ChevronTexaco and two or three other Western companies continue to believe that the project may be economically viable, but they are reluctant to move the project ahead without a green light from President Kuchma. The completion of the Druzhba-Adria pipeline in 2005 may breathe new life into the project because it might be even more efficient to send oil from Odessa to Brody to a spur of the Druzhba line. The game is not over, but at this point the Russians are far ahead in locking up their monopoly of east-west pipelines.

Electricity: The "Liberal Empire"

Anatoly Chubais, one of the original oligarchs of the Yeltsin era and the director of Russia's electricity monopoly, UES, was one of the most vocal supporters of the free market within Russia's business elite. During his several years at the helm of UES, he has repeatedly talked about breaking up the company into smaller units and privatizing the whole electricity system, including power generation and transmission and distribution lines. Beginning in mid-2002, however, his tone changed. He began expressing an interest in building UES into a business "champion" for Russia. He is now well known for his statement that he intends to build UES into a "liberal empire."

Chubais is particularly keen for UES to control all the power systems of countries that were once part of the Soviet Union or members of the Warsaw Pact. In September 2003, he claimed that he had "restored the common technology space in energy."[80] He added that, during the Soviet period, 11 national energy systems had operated together, but now UES was in control of 14 national networks, all directed from his headquarters in Moscow.[81]

Chubais bragged about UES's domination of the Belarusian, Armenian, and Georgian markets; talked about plans to take over the electricity systems in the three Baltic states, Slovakia, and Bulgaria; and claimed that the company was moving vigorously into the Turkish, Ukrainian, Kazakh, and Tajik markets. In an interview in September 2003, Chubais crowed about how his company's acquisition had put "the Georgian economy today in the hands of our company"; he went on to say that "the next step is to take over the Armenian energy sector. . . ."[82] In a later

80. "Press Conference with RAO UES of Russia Chair of Board Anatoli Chubais," Federal News Service, September 17, 2003.

81. Although Chubais counted the three Baltic states as within his system, the Baltic countries view themselves as in only a loosely coordinated network with UES.

statement, Chubais said, "Our target is not just ownership of stakes, but participation in the privatization of [other foreign] companies and eventually the acquisition of controlling stakes [in those companies]."[83]

Chubais confirmed that he had bought shares in Ukraine from President Kuchma's son-in-law, Viktor Pinchuk, and from the powerful business leader, Konstantin Grigorishin. UES expects to own 10 of Ukraine's energy-distributing companies by mid-2004. The UES purchase of Ukraine's electricity system was strongly and publicly opposed by Ukraine's minister of fuel and energy, Sergei Yermilov; Kuchma subsequently fired Yermilov in May 2004.

82. "TV Interview with RAO UES of Russia Chair of Board Anatoly Chubais," *Vremena*, September 29, 2003. In 2002, the Armenian government handed over a power plant to UES as payment for debts.

83. Alla Startseva, "UES Moves into Ukraine, Buys Stakes in 10 Power Distributors," *Moscow Times*, December 5, 2003.

Western Companies and Russian Monopolies

The monopoly power of Russia's companies in East Central Europe has by and large deterred Western competitors from attempting to enter the region's energy markets in any area except the retail trade. Western energy companies' generally negative linking with Russian partners during the 1990s has discouraged all but the largest firms from attempting to form joint ventures with Russian companies doing business in Central Europe.

Many of the Western energy firms that went to Russia in the 1990s ended up victims of asset stripping by their Russian partners. Most companies resolved not to return, but some firms have entered into joint ventures once again. One example is BP, which has taken the plunge and entered into a joint venture with TNK, its original asset stripper. Even so, one non-Russian TNK-BP executive in Moscow has observed that BP had discovered a greater "corporate culture divide" between it and TNK than BP had imagined when it agreed to the joint venture in 2002. Western energy firms have entered into some small strategic alliances with companies in Poland, Finland, Germany, and the Baltic states, but, except for Ruhrgas, most European companies have been reluctant to make major commitments in situations that rely on a Russian partner for all of the raw material.

ExxonMobil is an example of a large U.S. firm that recently had its previously approved exploration rights to the Sakhalin III field arbitrarily taken away by the Putin government, which appears determined to turn the field over to a more compliant Russian or foreign firm. The move against ExxonMobil occurred only a few months after the Putin government effectively killed an offer by the company to purchase 38 percent of YUKOS. ExxonMobil had been in talks with YUKOS for at least four years and conducted the first company-to-company discussions regarding the possibility of a production-sharing agreement (PSA). According to Exxon officials, negotiations for a PSA stopped only after Putin backed a change in Russian law that gave the "KGB-controlled Rosneft" an automatic blocking share in any PSA agreement with a foreign firm.

A relatively new problem has emerged that can sour Western investment in Russia's oil companies. On May 31, 2004, *Vedomosti* reported that Russian counterintelligence officials are questioning TNK's deal with BP because such a deal gives foreign executives access to information about the location and reserves of Russian oil fields—both are considered to be state secrets by the FSB.[84] One prominent Russian foreign policy observer stated that the TNK-BP merger caught the

---

84. Irina Reznik et al., "FSB Boitsia Utechki Gostain," *Vedomosti,* May 31, 2004, p. A1.

siloviki off guard and that Kremlin approval was rushed through by business-oriented members of the PA before influential former intelligence officers understood the implications of the joint venture. BP executives are nervously following this Kremlin debate between the intelligence interests and the business-oriented people. BP is concerned about the impact that restricting field information will have on its own operations, and it also fears that these restrictions will deter other potential Western investors, leaving BP more exposed politically to the suspicions of the Russian intelligence community.

In September 2004, Russia's minister of natural resources warned BP that the government might withdraw a production license for the Kovytka area that had been granted to the company. Some observers speculate that the new Gazprom-Rosneft conglomerate wants a larger role for itself in the area. This indicates once again to foreign energy investors that they are at the mercy of an arbitrary and overly suspicious bureaucracy and *siloviki*-influenced leadership that is convinced that benefits accruing to a foreign company must be at the expense of Russia itself.

In a recent case, the FSB warned an independent Russian energy company against hiring a former U.S. military officer; the reason given was national "security." In light of the current suspicion of foreigners that Putin and the siloviki are stirring up—Putin again linking energy and national security—it is no surprise the job offer was withdrawn.

Some Russian and foreign economists working in Moscow have recently speculated, however, that the growing personal relationship between Putin and Chancellor Gerhard Schröder and President Jacques Chirac will result in German and French firms receiving permission by the Kremlin to buy into attractive assets such as Sibneft, Sidanco, and YUKOS (after its expected reorganization). The economists assert that the French and Germans have subdued their criticism of the war in Chechnya and supported relatively easy terms for WTO accession in the expectation that Total, Gas de France, Ruhrgas, and ION will receive preferential treatment as foreign investors in Russian energy.

Not only do Russia's energy companies have the advantage in Central Europe of controlling enormous quantities of oil and gas reserves, but for the past several years they have also been better financed than many Western competitors. After the collapse and some particularly bad Western investments—Total's acquisition of a major refinery in the eastern part of Germany comes to mind—this situation became more pronounced. Also, Russian state companies such as Transneft, Gazprom, and LUKOIL carry very little debt. Private firms such as YUKOS, Rosneft, and TNK that were established by dubious privatization were able to acquire enormous assets, and whatever debt they incurred was usually owed to in-house banks, owned by the company's owners. Russian energy companies—both state companies and private firms—have been able to survive currency fluctuations, stock market slumps such as occurred in Russia in August 1998, and the kind of business crises that affected the U.S. energy companies in 2001–2002.

The major exception to foreign partnering during the past few years has been in the natural gas area. Gazprom knows it controls all or almost all of the imported natural gas supply in Central Europe; therefore, inclusion of a Western partner in some of its foreign investments does little to weaken its hold over the local gas industry. At the same time, joint ownership provides some reassurance to the host country that there is a counterweight to complete Russian control. In almost all instances, Gazprom's partner of choice has been Germany's Ruhrgas.

All three Baltic states and Poland perceive that Ruhrgas is very much the junior partner in any linkup with Gazprom, and that those governments do not expect Ruhrgas to oppose Gazprom activities that are clearly corrupt or constitute political interference in the host country. Ruhrgas's exclusion from the 15-year Russia-Ukraine gas deal has left the Germans disappointed.

The view among foreign energy experts in Moscow is that Putin appointed Alexei Miller as Gazprom's chief executive officer not to reform the company as was first announced. It appeared that Putin wanted the firm to be more aggressive in acquiring foreign market share and in assuring control over gas pipelines and gas infrastructure in Central Europe, the Caucasus, and Central Asia and over pipeline routes to China and Japan. The recently announced intent to merge Gazprom with Rosneft will strengthen Gazprom's and the state's influence in the energy sector.

As described earlier, the attempt of Williams of the United States to buy a majority share of Lithuania's facilities required the Americans to reach a supply agreement for crude oil with a major Russian oil company. At the same time, however, a LUKOIL executive remarked privately: "We [Russians] built the facilities with Russian money, and they should belong to us, not to the Americans."[85] Implied in the statement is the view that the facilities should not have even been considered the property of the Lithuanians. A senior official of LUKOIL made two trips to Lithuania in 1997 and 1998 to warn the Lithuanian government that LUKOIL should be given the facilities at no cost in return for Lithuania receiving a stable supply of crude oil. Instead of negotiating seriously with Williams and the Conservative government in Vilnius, LUKOIL preferred to use its political influence and its ability to block the flow of oil as the way to keep out any foreign competitor.

The Europeans understood, particularly after the disastrous asset stripping that occurred in Russia during 1995–2001, that the business cultures of West Europe and Russia were still too different to warrant significant financial risks. Europeans also recognized that profit for the Russian company was often not the major motivation. The exception to this practice is BP, but, as noted beginning on page 22 and on page 54, that had some aspects of a forced marriage. All of the Russian firms had offshore subsidiaries in locations such as Cyprus, the Turks and Caicos Islands in the Caribbean, Luxembourg, and the Netherlands. Profits from operations outside of Russia were often considered the private cash cow of the company's executives, not of the shareholders. In addition, offshore accounts helped avoid the scrutiny of Russia's tax authorities. Russia's Ministry of Internal Affairs has stated that approximately 60,000 Russian-owned companies are listed among the international tax havens abroad.[86]

---

85. Russian LUKOIL executive, conversation with author, 1998.

86. Kari Liuhto, "Operations of Russian Firms Abroad: Some Evidence from the Internationalization of Two Russian Energy Giants" (paper presented at "Transition and Enterprise Restructuring in Eastern Europe," the second international conference of the Copenhagen Business School, Hillerod, Denmark, August 17–19, 2000), p. 2.

A stark example of Russian business practices occurred in Lithuania in 1999. Duke Energy of the United States was given a draft contract by a Lithuanian business leader in which the Lithuanian offered to help Duke secure a contract to construct an electricity power bridge from Lithuania to Poland in return for the payment of $20 million. Although the contract was presented to Duke by a third party, the numbered account in the Turks and Caicos Islands that was to receive the illegal payment was registered to LUKOIL. It was no surprise when Duke Energy representatives rejected the offer and promptly flew back to North Carolina. LUKOIL and its supporters in Lithuania may have hoped to scare off the U.S. company in the first place, leaving the project to themselves. On the other hand, it is possible that the LUKOIL representatives had little experience dealing with U.S. companies, particularly a company that felt bound by the U.S. Foreign Corrupt Practices Act, which holds top U.S. executives criminally liable for the kind of payment requested.

CHAPTER 8

The EU and Alternative Energy Sources in Central Europe

The United States has not had a well-formulated policy focused on countering the dubious business practices of Russia's energy companies. Nor has much attention been paid to the growing potential for these firms and the Kremlin to undermine the new political and economic systems that emerged from the collapse of communism in East Central Europe. U.S. policymakers have vigorously supported the efforts of U.S. companies to enter the markets as competitors or partners to Russian companies, but the U.S. government has failed to develop policies that would help its Central European allies minimize the economic and security risks of Russian energy domination.

The European Union

The EU's focus has been on increasing energy supplies from Russia instead of on the conduct of Russian companies in the region. Some EU countries, primarily Germany, France, and Italy, view Russia as the indispensable partner necessary for increased energy supplies, and they are concerned that Europe will have to compete with the United States for Russia's energy.

EU enlargement and the debate around a new constitution have diverted the European Commission's attention from some of the critical issues still confronting the new democratic states to the east. Individual European governments also still prefer to deal with Russia in a bilateral rather than a multilateral context, but interest in East Central Europe by some Western governments has actually declined over the past few years. For example, Denmark has closed its embassy in Kyiv and conducts its relations with Ukraine out of Moscow. Energy issues in the Baltic states, Poland, and Ukraine are not major agenda items of the EU, except if the security of supply to the states farther west, particularly Germany but increasingly France and Britain, could be in doubt. Other countries have their own energy agendas: Denmark, Sweden, and Finland are troubled more by the environmental danger that increased oil shipments out of the Barents Sea or northern Baltic Sea pose for their coastlines than they are by Baltic or Polish energy security.

Another serious concern about Russia within DG TREN is the attempt by UES to sign agreements for greater electricity exports with EU members when the energy itself is generated by unsafe nuclear plants. In general, the attitude within the commission is that the new member states are mature enough to look after themselves when it comes to conducting economic relations with Russia. A more reasonable point made by the commission is that the new members and Ukraine have the prime responsibility to put their own political houses in order and develop transparent systems; such reforms will limit the ability of Russia and other foreign governments to corrupt other countries' political systems.

Conversations with EU officials reveal, however, that the commission lacks an understanding of the extent to which Russian energy companies are already influencing government policies in many of the new member states or of the long-term damage this can do to the EU itself. Although such a policy would defy logic, one commission official mistakenly believed that the Baltic states raised tariffs on oil shipped by rail in an effort to force Russia to use the Baltic ports.[87] The Russian government is actually increasing rail tariffs in order to force Russian companies to ship through the BPS rather than Baltic ports. The United States is more concerned than the EU that former intelligence officers occupy high-level positions in Russia's most important business area; the commission is rather dismissive of these concerns because members view Russia as an "energy giant but a military pygmy." [88]

A few countries—Germany and France, for example—display a curious readiness to accept Russian claims that the Baltic states discriminate against ethnic Russians. As a result, some European officials too easily dismiss Baltic warnings that Russia and its companies are interfering in their internal affairs. One EU official stated that the EU felt little willingness to help Latvia get piped oil from Russia to the port of Ventspils because of Latvian treatment of Russian minorities.[89] This attitude persists despite Council of Europe and OECD support for Latvia's claims that its treatment of ethic Russians complies with European standards. Another EU official said that the commission was not concerned with the Russian policy of bypassing the Baltic states and Poland as it builds new pipelines because the commission can understand Moscow's fears that the Baltic states may attempt to cut off supply routes if Russia adopts a policy that is "too supportive of ethnic Russians."[90] This type of alleged action on the part of the Baltic states has never taken place, and it is almost inconceivable that Baltic leaders would adopt policies so damaging to their own vulnerable economies.

The main focus of the EU is on east-west pipeline construction, particularly in light of the rapid depletion of the oil and gas fields in the United Kingdom. In addition, the clean air requirements of the Kyoto Treaty will require cutbacks in coal use. The EU is attempting to engage Russia and Ukraine in a dialogue over pipelines. The European Commission, to its credit, has established the INOGATE (Interstate Oil and Gas Transport to Europe) program, which provides technical assistance to the oil and gas sectors in the Caucasus and Central Asia, with the goal of increasing the secure supply of energy to EU countries. Although the focus has been on increasing Russian and Caspian crude oil and gas shipments to West European markets, the enlargement of the EU has increased the importance of the project for the new members. Unfortunately, INOGATE's worthy goal appears to be

---

87. EU DG TREN official, conversation with author, Brussels, January 2004.
88. EU official, conversation with author, Brussels, January 2004.
89. EU DG TREN official, conversation with author, Brussels, January 2004.
90. Ibid.

trumped often by political relations between Russia and the large member states, whether over the issue of Odessa-Brody or the building of the North Europe pipeline under the Baltic Sea.

Some in the United States and Europe mistakenly believe that NATO membership for Russia would eliminate any military threat from the East and that Russia's integration into the EU would protect post-Communist economies from the kind of economic pressure they faced from Russia in the early 1990s.

Ukraine, not an EU member, has brought a different set of issues because of its unique strategic position, size, and ethnic and historic ties with Russia. Ukraine was, through much of the 1990s, the largest per capita recipient of Western aid. By mid-2002, however, political corruption, arms sales to dubious recipients, and a weak sense of nationhood in Ukraine had led to a sense of donor fatigue and discouragement in the United States and Europe regarding prospects for Ukraine's integration into the West.

Nuclear Power

The Chernobyl nuclear disaster still reverberates politically in the West, particularly in Western Europe. The disaster only increased Western opposition to nuclear plants in other former Communist countries, whether they are of the Chernobyl-type RBMK design or not. The perception persists in Western Europe that the design and operation of all Soviet-built nuclear power plants automatically pose a danger of widespread nuclear contamination. Europe does not, however, have sufficient leverage over Russia to force closure of older Russian plants or even to compel the installation of modern safety systems in Russian nuclear plants. UES is still able to sell abroad electricity that originates in nuclear plants that do not come close to meeting Western safety standards.

The EU has considerably more influence over the nuclear power policies of the new EU members that possess Soviet-constructed plants than it does with Russia itself. The EU has insisted that all Soviet-constructed RBMK reactors in the new member states be shut down within the next 5–10 years. Denmark, Germany, and Austria have insisted that all Russian reactors, including those in the Czech Republic, Hungary, and Bulgaria, be closed almost immediately. Although the European Commission has promised generous grant assistance for replacing electricity supplies of the affected countries—Lithuania and Ukraine, in particular—the EU has yet to come up with funding sufficient to replace the electricity to be taken off-line with the closure of Soviet-era nuclear reactors.

The long-term effect of EU nuclear energy policies will be to increase the dependence of Poland, Lithuania, Latvia, Estonia, and Ukraine on oil and gas imports from Russia. There is certainly no inclination within the EU to provide subsidized Norwegian or Danish oil or gas imports to provide alternatives to energy supplies from Russia, even though the EU itself requires that at least 30 percent of a country's energy commodity be from a second source. The Poles were hoping for EU financial help to build a Baltic gas pipeline to bring in Norwegian gas, but they were rebuffed by the commission. The EU is aware that Gazprom can always undercut the price of North Sea gas, and the commission staff has not been in a position to make a financial aid commitment on the grounds of energy security.

The EU's environmental policies and its commitment to the goals of the Kyoto Treaty will work to undercut any attempt by the commission to help Poland and the three Baltic states achieve greater energy independence or even a diversification of their sources of imported energy. EU environmental policies will force future cutbacks in Estonia's oil shale production, Latvia's use of peat for heating, and Poland's use of coal. Latvia is considering importing coal from Poland to use in new, more efficient power plants, but EU environmental regulations will probably not permit this as a long-term alternative.

Barring a major investment in clean-coal technology, Ukraine will have to cut back on coal use for power plants and submit its Soviet-era and post-Soviet-era nuclear plants to tighter EU inspection if the country wants to join the EU. Some members of the EU are already unhappy that Ukraine is completing two nuclear plants that were started during the final years of the Soviet Union. These plants are safer and more efficient than the RBMK reactors that they replace, but they are not as secure as the Framaton reactors recommended by the European Bank for Reconstruction and Development (EBRD). Ukraine, however, continues to hope for more than the $250 million pledged by the EU for security upgrades.

Officials in Ukraine and Lithuania would like to see the EU carry out a scientific and rigorous study of the slim odds of a nuclear accident at a safety-enhanced RBMK reactor compared with the more likely disruption in supply that a political cutoff of energy from Russia would inflict on the new countries' economies.

Overall, EU policies are likely to push the five countries toward greater dependence on Russia, at least over the medium term.

Natural Gas

Another concern for the Central Europeans is the increasingly cozy relationship between Gazprom and the major gas companies of Germany—Ruhrgas and E.ON—and Gas de France. Some Central Europeans complain that Germany and France are naive to believe that their companies' alliances with Gazprom will provide sufficient protection against an increasing energy reliance on Russia. Undoubtedly, Russia would be much more reluctant to use the power of its energy supplies

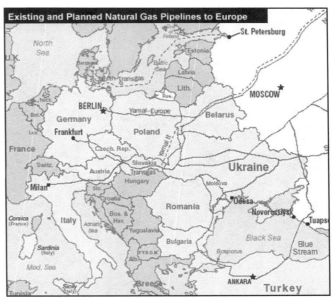

Source: U.S. Department of Energy, Energy Information Administration.

against the richer France and Germany than against countries that were once in the Soviet orbit. Unfortunately, neither Germany nor France has seriously attempted to restrain the corrupt and nontransparent practices of Russia, in either WTO or EU-Russia negotiations. Moscow's announcement in early 2004 that it would increase, rather than decrease, the state's stake in Gazprom provides no reason to believe that EU policies will result in Russian companies—especially those with ties to industrial champions in Western Europe—becoming more independent of the state.

CHAPTER 9

In Pursuit of Energy Security

Transparency and Corruption

If Russia were clearly on its way toward an open, transparent, modern democratic state, with ethical corporate behavior enforced by an honest judiciary, the problems discussed here would quickly fade. In fact, this paper probably never would have been written. A mature democracy in Russia would demand greater transparency on the part of the state, including the power ministries and intelligence organs, and more ethical conduct and open accounting standards by the countries' business executives. A more democratic Russia would likely have more respect for the sovereignty and aspirations of it neighbors. Democracy requires a fair amount of tolerance for competing ideas, acceptance of a free media, protection of private property, an impartial judicial system, and less popular acceptance of corruption.

These ethics and values are only slowly coming to post-Communist Europe, and Putin's Russia shows few signs of the same level of improvement that East Central Europe has experienced. Transparency in Russia is, however, greater than it is in most of the former Soviet republics of the Caucasus and Central Asia, but that is little comfort to Poland, the Baltic states, and most of Ukraine.

Russian nongovernmental organizations (NGOs) that press for transparency and anticorruption measures are under increasing pressure from the Kremlin to cease their operations or become tools of the government. Media figures who have written about corruption by individuals close to the Kremlin, within the intelligence services, or by high-level executives of state-owned or -controlled companies are silenced. Russia's neighbors, more than countries in any other region, have everything to gain by democratization and transparency in Russia. If Putin were to reverse his present course of acquiring vertical state control over Russia's natural resources sector and over alternative centers of political influence, the long-term political threat from Russia's energy monolith would diminish. Signs out of Moscow, however, do not point to a reversal of Putin's current policy. Putin's societal model appears to be closer to China's than to any European state's. Thus, Russia's energy policies must be examined in light of this disappointing situation.

Real privatization of Russia's energy companies, including the breakup of Transneft into competitive units, would reduce the ability of the Kremlin to use Russian companies to assert political control over its smaller and weaker trade partners. If the only goal of corporate Russia were to maximize profit for shareholders and if corporations had to use open, modern accounting systems, competition within Russia by private energy companies would reduce the ability of the Russian government to use Russian companies to gain political influence over neighbor states. Privatization would also ameliorate the more immediate danger to the new democracies—the spillover of corruption from official and corporate Russia.

Nevertheless, early transformation is not in the cards. The three Baltic states, Poland, and Ukraine will have to invest considerable resources of their own in order to ensure a greater degree of energy independence.

The first option of these states is political. Countries such as Ukraine and Lithuania must decide on the degree of ownership control they will cede to Russian oil and gas interests. Greater political and financial transparency in Ukraine and Lithuania might result in increased demands that Russian energy companies stop trying to influence decisions on privatization through campaign contributions and under-the-table payments to local political leaders. Membership in the EU for Poland and the Baltic states is no guarantee of good governance although it should help over the long run. The controversy surrounding protested elections in late 2004 may indicate that institutional reform and greater transparency may finally become a priority in Ukrainian politics.

The search for a solution will depend on the degree of real democracy and business transparency in each of the five countries. Where Russian companies and their supporters in the intelligence services have successfully co-opted the political elite, efforts to search for alternatives will be few. Before the presidency of Vladimir Putin, the Kremlin's foreign policy in East Central Europe was clumsy and heavy-handed and usually succeeded in stirring up resistance to Moscow's policies, even when it had the support of powerful members of the old *nomenklatura*. Putin, however, understands that a more subtle approach, with economic incentives for influential groups and the clandestine promotion of Russian power, is less likely to generate sufficient domestic opposition to thwart his plans. His well-publicized statement that Russia's activities abroad should take lessons from animals "whose ears do not show above the grass" expresses his inclination to use subversion in addition to persuasion.

An added concern is Putin's reluctance, or refusal, to carry through with his promises to stamp out official corruption. Control of Russia's road construction and railroad operations is in the hands of individuals handpicked by Putin who have a long history of corrupt practices.[91] Several respected observers, including Georgy Saratov, head of the think tank, INDEM, believe that corruption is growing rapidly under Putin, which may account in part for the government's determination to silence the country's best-known investigative journalists.

Government Pricing Policies

Domestic energy prices in Russia are cheap by world standards, a fact that reflects a long history of government subsidy, great resource availability, and low extraction costs. Since the collapse of the Soviet Union, there has been only slow progress in introducing metering systems that show how much energy is being used by a company for production or services or by a household for home heating. The absence of

---

91. Uwe von Klussmann, "Perfide Doppelstrategie," *Der Spiegel*, June 7, 2004.

metering also leads to arbitrary taxes and bribes—some call it flexibility—in assessing costs or levels of production.

The Baltic states, Poland, and Ukraine once also made use of such flexibility, although all five countries have, with varying degrees, modernized their metering and monitoring systems. Their energy costs, like Russia's, are serious domestic political issues, as one would expect in relatively poor countries located in one of the colder areas of the temperate zone.

Although possibly in conflict with EU regulations or WTO obligations, a degree of national control could be gained in East Central European countries if governments assessed slightly higher taxes on imported oil, gas, and electricity that originate in Russia. Some increase in domestic prices could provide incentives to look for more secure sources of energy, either domestic or foreign. For example, Norwegian gas or a new nuclear power plant might be economically attractive if Russian imports were taxed at even 5 percent. Such taxation could also encourage the faster introduction of energy efficiency measures in a region notorious for its energy waste. Russia and its companies that now control energy facilities in the five states would protest and might threaten retaliation; if Russia took strong action, the governments could offer to roll back their taxes if Russian companies agreed to binding arbitration in the West and the payment of stiff penalties for any disruption in supply.

Other Nontechnical Solutions

The EU should state that any Russian energy firms that have in the past arbitrarily cut off supplies to Central European countries could be forced by the EU to pledge some of their assets in the West as collateral so that a court could order their seizure in case of noncompliance with an arbitration decision. Although Russian companies would fight this measure, the threat from the EU would by itself signal that arbitrary blockages would not be tolerated in the future.

A measure of this kind would not directly help Ukraine; the EU could require Russia to sign the EU's Energy Charter, which requires the parties to be more transparent and competitive in their business dealings with member state companies. Transneft should be required to give up its monopoly pipeline to the West and, along with Gazprom, should be made to allow other gas companies to use its pipeline system, particularly in the case of spare capacity.[92]

Convincing Russia to sign the Energy Charter could be the most important single step the European Commission could take to help the Central Europeans. The Baltic states and Poland should be taking a greater role in the EU-Russia energy dialogue in order to push the European Commission to take a firmer position vis-à-vis Russia on the Energy Charter. The newer EU members should be advocating common EU policies on Russian power supplies and on defining supply criteria. For example, the commission should have a clearer policy on Russia's dumping of cheap electricity, which Russia offers to prevent the entrance into the market of

---

92. This is essentially the system that governs pipeline operations in the United States.

alternative suppliers. DG TREN could deal with the issue of Gazprom setting up daughter companies that are designed primarily to help fund local business and political interests.

The five target countries could work more closely with the International Energy Agency (IEA) in addition to their efforts with the EU. One energy expert in Washington has stated, "The key to disruption response is to act in concert with other [EU] members, the IEA, etc."

Baltic Technical Cooperation

At the initiative of the Baltic Council, representing the three Baltic states, the Baltic Council of Ministers established a coordination unit on energy in early 2002 to devise regional solutions to domestic energy shortages primarily in Estonia, Latvia, and Lithuania. Its goal is to introduce greater energy efficiency in the wider Baltic region. Among projects examined by the unit is the Baltic ring electricity grid, an electrical power bridge linking Lithuania and Poland, as well as scholarships for young professionals in the field of energy. Also included is a comprehensive analysis of fuel storage stocks and the handling of hazardous materials. Although the coordination unit first focused its attention on cooperation between the three Baltic states and the Nordic countries of Denmark, Finland, and Norway, it has now drawn in Poland, Russia, Germany, and the European Commission represented by DG TREN. A good number of studies are generated by the unit, but none of the projects under discussion has yet been implemented. The U.S. government should work closely with the EU coordination unit and offer technical assistance where appropriate.

The concept of a power bridge between Poland and Lithuania was proposed in the late 1990s as a way to sell excess electricity generated in Lithuania to Poland and, possibly, Germany. At the time, Lithuania was generating an excess of power, in large part through the operation of its two nuclear plants at Ignalina and the Kronas hydro unit in Kaunas, where one end of the power bridge was to be located. The project had not yet started when it became evident that the EU was going to demand a firm commitment from Lithuania to decommission its two nuclear reactors as a condition for the country's membership in the EU. The power bridge project could never attract the necessary Western technical or financial backing.

Beginning in 2002–2003, Lithuanians who were worried about their looming power deficit came to view power cable linkage as a means of bringing excess Polish electricity to the Baltic states during periods of domestic shortage in Lithuania and Latvia and of exporting power to Poland in periods of overcapacity. Lithuanians now believe that the EU has an obligation to help finance, or find financing, for a 1,000 megawatt transmission line in exchange for the closing of their nuclear reactors. The EBRD and EU are now seriously considering providing the five-to-seven-year project with the necessary funding and technical support although concerns have been expressed about possible environmental damage along the proposed route. Final approval of the project by the EU and EBRD has been held up by uncertainty surrounding the date for decommissioning Lithuania's Ignalina II reactor.

Complicating the project are allegations of corruption by Polish business interests that would benefit financially.

Storage and Redundancy

Poland and the three Baltic states are now covered by the EU requirement that they eventually have in storage stocks of crude oil and/or petroleum products sufficient to cover 90 days of domestic demand in the event of a supply shutoff. Such a stockpile would give the Baltic states a high degree of security from the kind of politically motivated supply disruptions caused by Russian actions as recently as April 2004. The costs will be substantial, and at least a decade will pass before the Baltic states can fulfill the EU's storage requirements.

All five of the countries have programs to increase their stocks of oil, although in some cases the storage will be owned and operated by the Russian companies supplying the crude stocks for emergency use. This could be an advantage to the host country if the storage acts, in effect, as collateral for the smooth supply of crude from Russia. Of course, the host country must also have access to the stocks, be able to monitor storage levels, and be able to decide circumstances under which the stored crude would be released into the domestic market. So far, none of the countries dependent on Russian storage on their territory seems prepared to insist on these conditions. A Ukrainian economist remarked recently that perhaps long-term foreign domination creates a mentality of dependence, which makes it easier for states that were once part of the Soviet Union to accept Russian insistence that it be done Russia's way. In this case the EU could help ensure host-country access to storage by foreign companies.

Natural gas storage is becoming increasingly important as natural gas continues to gain in share of power production. Although the EU has not issued a binding rule for the storage of gas, as it has for oil and oil products, it has strongly recommended that member states "take the necessary measures to ensure that consumers who are unable to switch to alternative fuels, such as gas, will continue to be supplied" for 60 days in the event of a disruption in supply and for as long as necessary in the event of extremely low temperatures or cold winters. The EU does not require that storage of oil or gas be on the territory of the country itself. The member state, however, must have unimpeded access to the supply in time of need.

Poland is favored with large underground caverns in the West and South of the country that are well suited for gas storage. Poland would also like to be a gas storage area for Germany, Slovakia, and possibly the Czech Republic. Filling the storage tanks or underground caverns, however, will in the short term increase reliance on Gazprom. If Gazprom moves forward with its announced plan to build its next pipeline to Europe under the Baltic Sea rather than parallel to Yamal I, it may only lengthen Poland's dependence on Gazprom for supply and continue to give considerable pricing power to Gazprom, even if the Russian company participates in the construction of new underground storage facilities.[93]

Gazprom must consider that if it ignores storage projects, it may allow future clout to West European companies that are interested in building additional storage capacity in Poland. If Poland were a larger transit route to Europe for Russian gas, Warsaw would have greater leverage with Moscow—a possible reason that Putin is supporting the Baltic Sea gas bypass. If demand for Russian gas grows substantially in Europe during the next few years, Gazprom could be forced to construct the cheaper Yamal II line in addition to the undersea route. Because energy security is already on NATO's agenda, perhaps NATO could examine the economic and security implications of Primorsk versus the Baltic ports and of the Baltic Sea gas pipeline versus Yamal II.

Latvijas Gaze owns an underground gas storage facility that has a current capacity of 4 billion cubic meters and can be expanded to 5 billion cubic meters. Gazprom already has partial ownership in Latvijas Gaze and intends to raise its stake to more than 34 percent, giving it a blocking share in the venture. Because Itera has another 25 percent, the two companies already have effective control over Latvijas Gaze. Press reports from Moscow state that in 2005 Lithuania plans to start building natural gas reserves in the amount of 300–500 million cubic meters.[94] Here again, Gazprom has 34 percent of the company and, with support from other friendly shareholders, expects to control the storage units.

The EU is pressing all its members to increase the use of renewables. Estonia's goal is for the share of renewables to be more than 5 percent of total electricity production by 2010, and 20 percent in cases where power and electricity are coproduced. It is expected (or, more likely, hoped) that the three Baltic states can achieve their goals through a combination of wind, hydropower, and biomass. The Baltic states share this goal but wonder who will provide them with the financing and technology to meet these targets. Some EU money will be made available as incentives for renewably produced power (18 billion euros over 20 years). Nevertheless, this money is to be spread among at least 13 countries, and the average EU-backed development project takes approximately 10 years to implement.

Danish and Swedish companies have already been involved in some financing of wind power and biomass for power generation, but most energy economists do not see realistic alternatives to fossil fuel or nuclear power over the next 10–15 years. Nevertheless, the European Commission should be given credit for setting firm, even if difficult to reach, standards for the less-developed member states.

Politics of Alternatives

Several projects will encourage East Central Europe to work together to achieve somewhat more energy independence. The most positive support from outside the region is coming from the Nordic states, which understand the long-term risks of Russian energy monopoly more clearly than do organizations farther removed from the region. The EU's INOGATE program is a good start, but the commission possesses too little political will to push back against Moscow's determined effort to

93. "Gazprom Negotiates on Construction of Underground Gas Storage Facility Worth $150 Million in Poland," *Russian Oil and Gas Report*, April 9, 2004.

94. "Lithuania Plans to Build 100 mln Euro Natural Gas Reservoir," Prime-TASS News Agency, March 19, 2004.

control all pipelines going westward. Russia's signature on the EU's Energy Charter would help, but again the large members of the EU are more interested in securing increased supplies of Russian oil and gas for themselves than in protecting the new members against Russian monopolies and unethical trade practices. A substantial commitment of EU resources to alternative sources of energy and/or additional help in building nuclear power plants might provide a greater measure of bargaining power for the Baltic states and Poland in their energy relationship with Russia. An EU-financed a pipeline to bring North Sea gas under the Baltic Sea to Poland would provide Poles with an emergency alternative, one that could easily be extended to Lithuania.

The situation in Ukraine is more complex. Most Ukrainians do not see a significant threat to national security in large-scale Russian ownership of their country's energy infrastructure. When asked about nationality (as distinct from citizenship), many Ukrainians state that they are the same as Russians. In addition, the country's political leadership has been, to some degree, an integral part of Russia's energy ownership complex in Ukraine. President Kuchma, his son-in-law, many members of his administration as well as the energy leadership hold shares in the same energy facilities. This does not mean, however, that Ukraine's leaders will allow Russian companies to swallow all Ukraine's energy assets. The desire of Ukraine's present leadership to maintain control of many of the country's energy assets is not motivated by concern over Russian domination but by a desire to capture for themselves a large share of the proceeds from an enormously profitable industry. Leaders who have had serious concerns about the political implications of Russian energy domination have been gradually forced out of the Ukraine government. The results of the December presidential election, however, should reverse this trend.

CHAPTER 10

The U.S. Policy Response

Constraints on U.S. Policy

Being 62 percent dependent on foreign oil and relying on imports of natural gas for 17 percent of its domestic consumption, the United States, like the EU, is searching anxiously for additional energy sources abroad that lie outside the volatile Middle East. U.S. consumption of energy per capita is the highest in the world: with 3 percent of the world's population, the United States consumes 20–25 percent of the world's oil.

In addition, the United States has a particularly weak energy conservation program. Little support exists for creating tax incentives or tax penalties that would substantially reduce domestic demand during the next few years. Issues of higher gasoline taxes and of significantly elevated fuel economy standards are off-limits to any politician with aspirations for national office. During spikes in international oil prices, the United States (as most developed countries) has little alternative but to appeal to the members of OPEC to consider possible damage to the world economy as well as the fact that sustained high prices might drive the search for nonoil sources of energy and thus reduce the demand for oil.

The U.S. government, along with U.S. energy companies, is therefore in the curious position of encouraging the Putin administration to export more oil and gas to international markets. This encouragement comes at the same time that the Putin government has been ambivalent about helping U.S. energy companies, including those that are proposing legitimate production-sharing agreements with Russian companies. Neither has Moscow been helpful to U.S. firms interested in buying shares in Russian companies, although ConocoPhillips's recent purchase of 7.8 percent of LUKOIL will be trumpeted by Putin as a welcome for U.S. companies—as long as they do not acquire sufficient shares for a controlling or blocking interest, of course. U.S. embassy sources in Moscow concede that the main focus of the U.S.-Russian bilateral energy dialogue—directed by subcabinet officials, with Deputy Prime Minister and Minister of Industry and Energy Viktor B. Khristenko and Vice President Richard B. Cheney following the discussions but not actively participating—is on a new Barents Sea port.

Some U.S. officials are concerned that Putin and his *siloviki* colleagues are deeply opposed to a long-term U.S. presence in the Caucasus and Central Asia and are determined to keep the U.S. corporate presence and influence in the region to a minimum. These officials also fear that Russia is slowly moving toward closer cooperation with OPEC on production levels and price goals. Since late 2003, OPEC officials have been more active in trying to enlist Moscow's cooperation. Greater Russian cooperation with OPEC and the higher resulting oil prices would also damage the weaker, more energy-intensive, and less energy-efficient economies of East Central Europe.

U.S. companies are instead competing intensively with European firms for favor in the Kremlin. As Russia's oil and gas reserves are increasingly controlled by the central government even if they are nominally owned by private shareholders, competition for ownership and exploration rights are being decided for political reasons more than for business reasons. Further complicating U.S. policy following the YUKOS shock are the increasing indications that Premier Mikhail Y. Fradkov is not in favor of widespread privatization or foreign investment in Russia's energy sector. The anxious competition between United States and other world leaders, notably France, to promote their countries' energy firms as investment partners for Russian companies has enfeebled the West's efforts to force more transparency on Russia's energy giants.

Any U.S. action to force transparency and real competition among Russian companies can be successful only if it is carried out jointly with the EU. Europe is already constrained from exerting pressure on the Kremlin to allow greater competition in pipeline routes from the Caspian Sea to Europe. The war in Iraq has also diminished the policy options of U.S. policymakers in dealing with Russia. The United States is also in constant competition with France and Germany for the Kremlin's support over strategy vis-à-vis Iraq and Iran and on counterterrorism policy. Europeans are also generally closer to Russia on the issue of trade sanctions, which reduces the U.S. ability to support the efforts of the five countries to limit, or roll back, the influence of Russian companies in their domestic policies.

Europeans recognize that Putin's Russia will not become a modern democratic state in the next few decades. Europeans, as much as Americans, are aware of the negative as well as positive steps that Putin has initiated. They rightly argue that they have more at stake in maintaining good relations with Russia—that geography gives Americans the luxury of taking a more detached view of Moscow's policies. It could be argued by Americans that this obliges Europeans to push the Kremlin harder to implement reforms that will make the entire European area more secure. If Europe and the United States are reluctant to force Russia to honor its commitments regarding troop withdrawals from Georgia and Moldova, pushing Russia to clean up its energy practices in Central Europe may be even more difficult.

An added problem ironically derives from the recent economic success of the target countries. GDP in Poland, Ukraine, and the three Baltic states is growing at 4–8 percent annually. This permits the United States to presume that the building of democracy and free markets is proceeding normally in Central Europe, with the exception of Ukraine, and that energy security issues are not an immediate problem.

Recommendations for U.S. Action

- The U.S. embassies in all five capitals should be tasked with thoroughly analyzing each country's degree of dependence on Russian oil, gas, and electricity imports.

- The embassies could do the studies jointly with the local EU representatives. Up to now, neither the United States nor the EU has collected much intelligence on the activities of Russian energy companies or of Russia intelligence services' activities in East Central Europe. This information deficit has only grown as the West has focused increasingly on issues such as terrorism, weapons of mass destruction, and high energy prices.

- After the in-country studies have been completed, a team of analysts familiar with Russian energy policy assembled from various branches of the U.S. government should be sent to the five countries. The team would be tasked with determining the extent to which Russian companies are used by the Russian government as agents of state influence, the degree to which local business corruption is reinforced by Russia's energy companies, and whether U.S. and other Western energy companies are prevented from entering the market because of monopolistic or corrupt practices by Russian companies.

- The U.S. ambassador in each country would then submit an unclassified version of each country's report to the prime minister or appropriate local officials to request and solicit the views of the host government regarding the issue. The ambassador should first, however, determine the extent to which the country's leadership (including the top officials) is tied financially or otherwise to Russian companies or Russian government representatives.

- The U.S. mission to the EU should initiate high-level consultations with DG TREN to report on the findings of the U.S. government and to ascertain whether the EU is interested in carrying out joint discussions with the five countries on how to overcome areas of overdependence.

■ The U.S. Department of Energy and the U.S. Agency for International Development could develop a grant program for all East Central Europe countries more than 40 percent dependent on total Russian energy imports. This program would share at no cost to the participating countries findings of U.S. research and technology on energy efficiency and alternative energy sources. Clean coal, oil shale, and peat technology should be given precedence.

■ The U.S. government should initiate high-level consultations within NATO and with the EU over the dangers of overdependence by the Central Europeans on Russian energy monopolies, the security implications of this dependence, and measures to better manage the risks that are created.

■ The United States should initiate discussions within the IAEA, IEA, and EBRD that are not limited to safety or financial issues; these talks would instead look at the question of whether East Central Europe countries should be encouraged for national security reasons to assume higher domestic energy costs in order to diversify energy imports.

■ The United States should close its retail market to those Russian firms that do not practice transparency in their operations abroad or that have cut off energy supplies to one of the five countries in what was clearly the application of political or business pressure on the importing state. For example, LUKOIL is allowed to operate almost 1,000 retail gasoline stations in the United States and is negotiating to buy a U.S. refinery; at the same time LUKOIL is working closely with the Putin government to restrict U.S. energy firms from entering the Russian market.

- The United States should encourage the NATO secretary general and the president of the European Commission to quietly warn the Kremlin against using its energy companies to interfere in the domestic and security policies of the new Eastern European members of NATO and the EU.

- The United States and EU should push for real privatization—not pseudo-privatization—of Russian energy companies. They should demand a level playing field in Russia as the price of permission for Russian companies to own retail or refining facilities in the United States and Western Europe.

- The United States should work with the EU and Transparency International (TI) to secure greater business transparency in formerly Communist states. Publicize TI's ranking of each country's corruption level and highlight problem areas.

- The United States should initiate a NATO examination of the OECD-IEA sharing program designed to deal with import interruption to one of the member states. NATO and the EBRD could explore financing possibilities that would allow new members to reach more quickly the EU's strategic storage goals.

- The EBRD, with a push from the United States, should help Poland—believed to possess a considerable amount of unexploited natural gas—finance an increase in domestic gas production from 3 to 5 million cubic meters, thereby providing the country with 50 percent of its domestic consumption. The EBRD could assume a minority equity stake in the project until a suitable Western firm buys the EBRD share.

- At the urging of the United States and the EU, expensive regional projects—the Nordic-Baltic power grid, the Polish-Lithuanian power bridge, the Norwegian-Danish gas pipeline to Poland, or a longer extension of the present gas pipeline into Germany—could receive low-cost financing from the EBRD.

- The United States and Europe should actively encourage more inter-European interdependence in pipeline construction in order to lessen dependence on one supplier and decrease the risk in case of supply disruption.

- The United States should stop actively encouraging Russia to build pipelines quickly to the Barents Sea in order to ship oil and gas directly to North America. Russia should be left to decide whether the pipelines are in its own interest and not a response to Western energy shortfalls or fear of Middle Eastern instability. Actively promoting more pipelines diminishes U.S. leverage on Russia to make its companies operate with more transparency or create a more level playing field for U.S. companies trying to develop profitable business ventures with Russian companies.

■ The United States should join the EU in carrying out a dialogue with the new Ukrainian government, the Kazakhs, and the Western energy companies to find political and economic incentives that would increase the commercial attractiveness of completing a pipeline system that carries Caspian crude from the Black Sea to Europe via Ukraine and Poland—a system that does not provide Russia with the ability to disrupt shipments.

CHAPTER 11

Conclusions

The primary issue for Poland, Ukraine, Estonia, Latvia, and Lithuania is not whether they import large amounts of energy from Russia; their imports will remain an inevitable fact of geography and geology. Most important is how they use their complicated energy relationship with Russia to make their economic, political, and security risks more manageable. Because it would be quixotic to expect more democratic change—including greater political and economic transparency—to occur in Russia in the near future, transformation must be accelerated in the importing countries.

Institutions such as the OECD, World Bank, and IMF have pushed, with varying degrees of success, for greater transparency in government and for the adoption by all countries of internationally recognized accounting standards. Public pressure on Central European governments and on Russia to implement these measures might help reduce much of the corrupting effect in the relatively weak East Central European states, corruption reinforced by the most egregious interference of Russian energy and security interests. A more aggressive and better-trained independent media that is immune from government interference or foreign political interests could add much to the public's knowledge of domestic groups that are beholden to Russia's energy companies.

The U.S. government and the EU should stop and reconsider the costs—to themselves and to the Central Europeans—of their rush to secure additional oil and gas supplies from Russia. The dismantling of YUKOS, largely for political reasons, points up the risks of ignoring distinctions between Russian companies that are trying to become more Western in their corporate governance standards and those that remain enigmatic instruments of Russia's imperial inclinations. Competition for Russia's energy riches is understandable but should be tempered by recognition that corrupt Russian business practices are imported perforce along with their oil and gas supplies. Western governments should not appeal directly to Putin for increased production and exports; market forces should be the determinant.

Russian companies are eager to increase their markets and investments in the West. LUKOIL has been allowed to expand its operations in the United States and Western Europe—while it has worked diligently to prevent Western firms from acquiring an influential role in Russia's domestic market—although it has been tied repeatedly to corrupt practices in places as diverse as Iraq and Ukraine. The United States and the EU are in a strong position to demand greater openness and accountability from Russian firms wanting to enter their markets. Delay in responding to the challenge is the West's worst choice.

The refusal of Americans to adopt strong energy conservation measures and agree to mandatory reductions in gasoline consumption weakens the U.S. negotiating position vis-à-vis Moscow over the conduct of Russian companies abroad. Increasing oil imports gives greater power to OPEC and, indirectly, to Russia. The EU's unwillingness to insist that Russia sign the Energy Charter or to demand a higher degree of business transparency on the part of Russia's energy firms only encourages Moscow to use its companies to leverage political control over its neighbors. Shortsightedness on the part of the United States and the EU should not stop them from ensuring that Russian firms that operate within NATO or EU countries abide by Western business standards. Western governments should also not shrink from demanding a level playing field for their firms in Russia. Introduction of greater competition and transparency would of course work to the long-term advantage of Russia.

With the United States preoccupied with counterterrorism, Islamic radicalism, and weapons of mass destruction and the EU distracted by institutional enlargement, power allocation, and attempts by some to balance U.S. global power, it is understandable that Putin believes Russia has a free hand in promoting old imperial interests in areas as diverse as Chechnya, Ukraine, and Lithuania. Policy toward Russian energy activities in Ukraine is ineffective as long as Ukraine's political elite is in bed with Russia's energy barons.

The larger political issues surrounding the Kremlin's destruction of YUKOS— its most innovative and transparent energy company—should give pause to Westerners who interpret the YUKOS affair as a unique case in which the Russian state is merely confiscating the illegally secured assets of one of its best-known oligarchs. To the contrary, the YUKOS issue is about more than a struggle between Putin and Khodorkovsky or the alleged skirting of the tax laws by YUKOS.

The YUKOS affair is a timely demonstration of Putin's belief that the country's natural resources must be used to advance narrowly defined national security interests. By itself, Putin's policy is consistent with policies in democratic countries like Norway. Russia nevertheless differs because its national security interest, as defined by Putin and a large part of the power structure, is to establish decisive control over political and security decisionmaking in neighboring states. This Russian control is to be used to ensure that there are friendly governments in place that will support Russian security and economic interests. Calling Russian economic projection "imperialism" would be an exaggeration, but the neocolonial characteristics of Russia's foreign energy policy are apparent to those living in the neighborhood.

The United States should take the lead and work with the EU and the Central Europeans to analyze the political and security risks that stem from Russia's use of its energy companies as instruments to subvert and corrupt countries that were formerly within the security orbit of the Soviet Union. The United States and the EU should also collaborate to draw up an action plan to counter Russian energy policies that threaten the consolidation of democracy and free markets in Poland, Ukraine, Estonia, Latvia, and Lithuania. A more rapid consolidation of transparent democracy and open markets in East Central Europe would also have a significantly positive impact on the course of reform in Russia, Belarus, and Ukraine. Long-term security interests of the United States and its allies are therefore intimately tied to ensuring the failure of the cycle of corruption and imperial control that underlies Russia's foreign energy policy.

About the Author

Keith C. Smith is currently a senior associate in the CSIS Russia and Eurasia Program. Until recently, he served as a consultant for an international energy company. Ambassador Smith retired from the U.S. Department of State in 2000, where his career had focused primarily on European affairs. From 1997 to 2000, he was U.S. ambassador to Lithuania. His earlier posts in Europe included Hungary (twice), Norway, and Estonia, and in all three countries, he served as chargé d'affaires for extended periods. In addition to several other State Department assignments, he most recently served as director of policy for Europe, senior adviser to the deputy secretary of state for support of East European democracy (the SEED Program), and director of area studies at the Foreign Service Institute.